How to Be a Successful Teaching Assistant

Also available from Continuum

Louise Burnham: *101 Essential Lists for Teaching Assistants*
Janet Kay: *Teaching Assistant's Handbook*
Janet Kay: *Teaching Assistant's Handbook: Primary Edition*
Susan Elkin: *Teaching Assistant's Guide to Literacy*

How to Be a Successful Teaching Assistant

Jill Morgan

continuum

Continuum International Publishing Group
The Tower Building   80 Maiden Lane, Suite 704
11 York Road   New York, NY 10038
London, SE1 7NX

www.continuumbooks.com

© Jill Morgan 2007

Jill Morgan has asserted her right under the Copyright, Designs and
Patents Act, 1988, to be identified as Author of this work

British Library Cataloguing-in-Publication Data
A catalogue record for this book is available from the British Library.

ISBN: 0–8264–9328–9 (paperback)

Library of Congress Cataloging-in-Publication Data
A catalog record for this book is available from the Library of Congress.

Typeset by Kenneth Burnley, Wirral, Cheshire
Printed and bound in Great Britain by Ashford Colour Press Ltd,
Gosport, Hampshire

Contents

Contents

List of tables

List of figures

Introduction

The purpose and structure of this book

This book has been written for Teaching Assistants (TAs) – the many support staff who work in our schools and who are so critical to the success of the education system. Its purpose is to help TAs be successful in their assigned duties and responsibilities. Whether you work in a primary, secondary or special school, in classrooms or pupil referral units, if you are a TA, this book was written for you.

Why read this book?
This book will provide you with guidelines on how to be successful in your work as a TA. You will find two main aspects:

1. Knowing the details of your assigned roles and responsibilities.
2. Knowing how to work effectively with your supervising teacher or other professional.

These are the two major areas which you can work on to increase your level of success as a TA.

What do we mean by success? What sort of success do you think of when you see the title 'How to be a successful TA?' Take a moment to write your thoughts here.

For some people, success is a sense of autonomy, and being able to work independently. For others it may be more of a sense of being someone's 'right-hand man' and feeling indispensable. Others may see success only in terms of a pupil's successful performance, and not in relation to the TA's role in supporting that pupil. So the various definitions of success are quite personal, and – as you will find so often throughout this book – there may be no one right answer that will fit everyone's situation or preferences.

We can see success in terms of both what is there and what is lacking or absent. Let's deal with the lacks or absences first. In a very basic but important sense, success is a lack of conflict. Who can feel successful when there is tension or when there are negative interactions between people who work together? But there is also the tension of having a goal or aim in mind, and not being able to achieve it – such as might occur when you take a job that looks appealing but once you begin your work, you find that it is not what you had imagined. And then there is the tension and conflict that can build when areas of responsibility and lines of authority are unclear, making it difficult to know whether you are carrying out all your duties, and yet not overstepping the mark or taking on too many responsibilities. Perhaps then we can say that success – certainly in the workplace – is the presence of effective and purposeful activity, according to clearly understood expectations, in a supportive and caring atmosphere. Let's take a moment to examine this idea by breaking success into two parts; the presence of success and the lack of it.

Success is . . .

The presence of . . .	*A lack of . . .*
Harmony, collaboration	Conflict – tension and disagreement
Understanding, clear communication, a feeling of capability	Confusion
Achievement	Disappointment and failure
Learning applied to action	Failure to learn or failure to act
Effective teaching support	Failure to adequately support learning

---

If you look at the box, you can see that some of the items listed as contributing to success are linked to an end product – your own achievements and the success of your pupils – but most of them are concerned with process. They are not end results but part of the day-to-day environment in which you work, and the ways in which you carry out your responsibilities, rather than the product of your efforts. You might even think of this more in terms of job satisfaction. Some of the research on the success of those who work together as a team focuses on the team members' need to feel that they are achieving something (a product), but also to feel that they really belong to that team, and that they are making a contribution to its success – meaning that they are an important part of the very process.

As a TA, you are successful when you are performing your assigned duties, fulfilling your responsibilities to the best of your ability, and working well with your supervisor; in other words completing the tasks prescribed by your job description, and enjoying that powerful feeling that comes when you achieve personal goals.

> Coming together is a beginning. Keeping together is progress. Working together is success.
>
> *Henry Ford*

Regular features

A number of regular features have been included in this book to enhance the benefits of reading it. Throughout the book you will find examples of how you can put the theories into practice as well as guided-practice thinking opportunities – places in the text where you are asked to give your opinion or draw on your own experience. You may not wish to write on the book, in which case you can photocopy relevant pages and keep a loose leaf folder of papers relating to your reading and study, as a supplement to the book. Under the terms of copyright these copies can be made, but *only for your own use*.

In later chapters you will also find case studies involving TAs. These case studies are presented in several parts, and you will be asked to respond to each of the parts before moving on to the next. This format is meant to represent real life situations where we very rarely get all of the information we need at once, and where we often have to amend our opinions and decisions to accommodate new information. These case studies give you opportunities to stop and reflect on your learning, and apply the principles to real life situations.

At the end of each chapter you will find a self-evaluation exercise – *How well am I doing?* – so that you can take a look at where you are in relation to the principles discussed in the chapter and make plans for where to go next.

TAs in the UK and elsewhere

TAs can be found in all of the national education systems of the Western hemisphere as well as in the Antipodes. Canada, the United States and Australia all rely heavily on TAs to provide comprehensive educational services to pupils of school age. This has been true in these countries – as in the UK – for many decades now. In fact, strictly speaking, there were TAs in Britain even as far back as Victorian times, as the older and more able pupils were put to work as assistants to the teachers, and helped the younger or less able children with their lessons. They were known as pupil teachers, and your grandmother or great-grandmother may have been one. Some of them went on to become teachers themselves.

Fortunately you are now paid for the work you do, but at least some of the principles involved in using pupil teachers in late eighteenth century and early nineteenth-century classrooms still apply to your work as a TA:

- You pick up some of the teacher's responsibilities, so that he or she can attend to those that require the greatest expertise and cannot legally be delegated.
- You work under the teacher's direct supervision, as he or she assigns, monitors and evaluates your work.
- You learn from the work you do with pupils, and gain valuable experience about how classrooms work and what methods are most effective for ensuring that pupils learn.

Historically in the UK, TAs have been known by a variety of names – learning support assistants (LSAs), non-teaching assistants, paraprofessionals. The most recent terms adopted by governments include:

- Paraprofessional (USA)
- Teaching Assistant or Classroom Assistant (Canada)

- Teacher Aide (Australia)
- Teacher Aide, Classroom Assistant or *kaiaawhina* (New Zealand)

As you can see from the variety of titles in the box below, some of the titles are more descriptive than others. A title such as 'paraeducator' was suggested in the United States some years ago, to mirror the names given to paraprofessionals in other professions – such as paramedic and paralegal – but the US government chose to use the more generic term paraprofessionals in the 2001 and 2004 re-authorizations of major education legislation. Interestingly, in Scotland TAs are known as Classroom Assistants, because of a feeling that if they become known as Teaching Assistants, with an associated increase in status, they will become 'teachers on the cheap'. So the change to TA, in line with the rest of the UK, has been resisted. In some countries Teaching Assistants also work at University level – they are often graduate students who are helping to teach undergraduate classes – but our main focus in this book is on paid support staff who work in primary and secondary schools in the UK.

Titles used for TAs in English-speaking countries

Aide
Teacher Aide
Paraprofessional
Paraeducator
Paratherapist
Instructional Assistant
Classroom Assistant
Education Technician

According to the Department for Education and Skills (DfES) there were over 146,000 TAs in schools in England in 2005. This is a Full-Time Equivalent (FTE) number, and many TAs work part-time, so there were of course many more individual TAs than that number. As you can see from the table below, about two-thirds of these TAs worked in primary schools. In comparison, there were over 447,000 (FTE) teachers working in schools in England in 2005 – three times as many as TAs – but only 47 per cent of them worked in primary schools. And you will probably not be surprised to see from the table, that in special schools TAs outnumber teachers, not only in the percentage who work there but also in the actual numbers of TAs employed. So you can see that the distribution of teachers and TAs differs quite substantially. The number of TAs has been steadily increasing since 1997, when there were only about 61,000 in England, with a big increase occurring around 2004–5 with the government's workforce remodelling initiative. This increase in number of TAs is much larger than the increase in number of teachers over the same period of time.

Table 1.1: Teachers and TAs in schools in England in 2005

Stage	Number (and %)	
	TAs	Teachers
Primary schools	95,460 (65%)	204,840 (47%)
Secondary schools	29,980 (21%)	220,760 (50%)
Special schools	18,540 (13%)	14,900 (3%)
Pupil Referral Units (PRUs)	2,070 (1%)	6,520 (1%)
Total	146,050	447,020

In addition to TAs working in English schools, there are more than 13,000 TAs working in schools in Wales, and the Welsh Assembly allocated £33m in the 2004–5 budget for reducing teachers' workload, partly by employing larger number of TAs. In Scotland there are more than 7,500 TAs (called Classroom Assistants) just working in primary schools. You will not be surprised to know that more than 90 per cent of TAs in the UK are women. If you are interested in finding out more about TAs in other countries, you will find some useful websites in the appendix.

On being an adult learner

You may be reading this book as part of an assignment for a college course or other training provided by your Local Authority (LA). Or you may have bought the book because you liked the look of it and wanted to improve your own effectiveness as a TA. Whichever is the case, picking up this book and reading it makes you an adult learner. And that may be quite intimidating, especially if you left school after 'O' levels or GCSEs and have only been back since as a parent or because of your job as a TA. But consider some of the advantages of being an adult learner:

- You have life experience. Everything you read and hear, all the new information you acquire, can be placed in the context of years of experience in many different aspects of life. This type of contextual knowledge which you have gathered informally, is tremendously important and useful, even though you have no qualifications to show for it, and you may not really be aware of possessing it.
- You are no longer an adolescent. If you left school as a teenager, your most recent memories and experiences of school and learning were mixed up with the distractions of adolescence, with the hormones and the uncertainties. Hopefully you have dealt with those now. Even if you have exchanged your teenage uncertainties for those of adult life, you should now be in a position to see things more clearly than you could when you were last in school as a pupil.

That having been said, returning to study after a long break can be quite intimidating, and most adult learners feel some sense of apprehension, even though they may be eager to learn. Here are some of the things that adult learners often say, and some advice about each one:

- *I feel so stupid and ignorant – everyone else seems so clever!* Two things here. First, you are not a bit stupid, especially if you have decided to improve your skills and have already taken a step towards this by enrolling in a course or studying on your own. That sort of decision is smart and courageous. Second, our own thoughts and ideas often seem so obvious to us while other people's thoughts and ideas, on the other hand, can seem quite brilliant. Both of those views are too extreme to be true. Hopefully your studies will teach you to value your own thinking as well as other people's, and to treat new ideas for what they are – something to be interested in and chew over, no matter who generated them.

- *I've got no qualifications, so what do I know?* You may not have much by way of formal qualifications, but if you are open-minded and willing to learn you can be effective and successful in your work as a TA. Whether you have experience in the classroom or not, if you apply new knowledge and skills as you acquire them, you will be able to make the most of your practical classroom experiences. Formal study will help explain why you already do some of the things that you do in your classroom, and why your supervising teacher asks you to work in particular ways or use particular methods. You should find that you already know a lot of what you are about to read – at a certain level – but reading and studying further will improve your understanding and your confidence in your work.

- *There are things I don't understand but I'm afraid to ask silly questions.* If you read or hear something that you don't understand, then do ask your teacher or another colleague if they can help. The only foolish question is the one you don't ask. No teacher should object to being asked about teaching, and most teachers are only too happy to extend their favourite occupation to the adults they work with as well as the children.

These comments have been made by TAs everywhere, but remember that as an adult, you bring many life experiences that can enrich the classroom, so you have a great deal to contribute. As you read each of the chapters, you will have many opportunities to think about your own working situation and how you can improve your work. But you will also have opportunities to identify the skills and strengths you bring to your work, and the ways in which you can contribute to children's learning and to your collaborative efforts with your supervising teacher.

1

What is a TA?

In this chapter we look at what defines a TA:

- how the government views TAs;
- roles which are considered appropriate for TAs, and the provisions which have been made to ensure that TAs are well prepared for their responsibilities;
- how TAs fit into the education system;
- why we make the distinction between TAs and teachers or other education professionals;
- the standards which have been set for TAs' work;
- the formal qualifications which are available to TAs.

Each of these areas contributes to a better understanding of your role as a TA – the first of the two major areas which will help you to be successful in your work.

What is a TA?

Your personal definition

If you were asked the question 'What is a TA?' how would you respond? There are some countries, such as China, which only employ fully qualified teachers – they have no TAs. So if someone from China were to ask you 'What is a TA?' what would you say to them?

Activity: What is a TA?

Take a minute to write your thoughts in the box below.

Sometimes when we give a definition in this way, we tend to list what that person does. For example, a mechanic repairs cars, or an accountant manages financial records. If that is what you just did in your definition, try to add something to it, which would give a more general picture of the purpose of the TA's role, rather than just listing typical duties.

Activity

Why do we have TAs in schools? What educational purpose do they serve? Use the box below for any additional thoughts and ideas.

Official definitions

The umbrella term for TAs used by the government is 'support staff'. However, this also includes clerical and administrative staff, so the term 'Teaching Assistant' or 'TA' designates support staff whose responsibilities are linked directly to pupil learning. In the words of a Department for Education and Skills (DfES) document:

> The term 'Teaching Assistant' (TA) is used to refer to staff in England & Wales who work with teachers in classrooms supporting the learning process (primary, special and secondary schools). This includes those with a general support role and those with specific responsibilities for a pupil, subject area or age group. These staff have a range of job titles: teaching assistant, classroom assistant, learning support assistant, special needs assistant, welfare assistant. 'Teaching assistant' is the agreed generic term in England and Wales.

In 2000, the DfES sent a document to all schools entitled 'Supporting the TA: A good practice guide'. In that document it was suggested that although support for the teacher is the core of what TAs do, they provide four different types of support:

1. Support for pupils – that is, all pupils with whom they come into contact during the course of their working day, not just those they have special responsibility for.
2. Support for teachers, by carrying out routine tasks but also in more specialist teaching roles.
3. Support for the curriculum, especially in the areas of literacy and numeracy.
4. Support for the whole school, as they work as part of a team and promote the well-being of pupils and the school ethos.

As you can see, this provides us with a broad definition of what TAs are: staff who provide support to pupils, teachers, the curriculum and the whole school. This definition will acquire greater detail as we consider where TAs fit into the education system alongside teachers and other staff, and how the standards set for TAs' work shape the contribution they make. 'Supporting the TA: A good practice guide' also emphasized the need for TAs to receive support from the school, suggesting a mutually beneficial relationship between TAs and the rest of the school staff, but that is something we will look at in the later chapter on working with your supervisor.

You may feel that your role is made up exclusively of supporting an individual pupil, or providing general support for a teacher, but the four different aspects of a TA's supporting role really are impossible to separate. You may wish to think about the different ways you provide support in these four areas.

Activity

Using the diagram, write in things that you do to provide support in each area: support for the pupil, support for the teacher, support for the curriculum, and for the school.

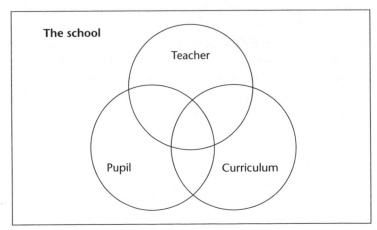

Figure 1.1: Providing support for the school, curriculum, staff and pupils

How do you fit into the education system?

Under the terms of the Education Act 2002, the legal responsibility for providing education to children lies with the government body, the Department for Education and Skills (DfES). The DfES fulfils this responsibility by authorizing various organizations (Local Authorities, grant maintained schools, private schools, etc.) to provide education services at a local level. This allows education to be tailored to meet local needs, and gives power to those who live in an area to make some of the education decisions for the children who live there. LAs pass authority down to schools to actually provide the day-to-day teaching, and this is the level at which most TAs work – supporting the class-level teaching process. Teaching Assistants can either be recruited by the LAs or by an individual school. These local employers also decide what skills, experience and qualifications are necessary for a particular TA post, although – as we will discuss later – the government has given guidance on the skills and knowledge that TAs should already have when they are first employed.

As a TA, you really do work at what is sometimes called the 'chalk face'. This is a rather outdated metaphor in this era of whiteboards and computers, but it does denote the very practical level at which you interact with the children whom the education system is designed to serve – in the classroom where teaching and learning are the focus of daily activities. The children are the clients of the education system, if you will. They should certainly be the major beneficiaries. All of the other levels of the system – national government departments, local authorities, laws and regulations at every level – provide a framework and resources so that teaching and learning can happen. And your involvement comes at that teaching and learning level.

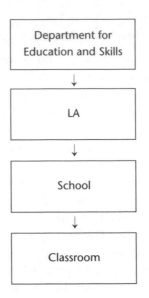

Figure 1.2: Levels in the education system

Why the distinction between TAs and professionals?

By law, schools are required to employ a qualified teacher for every class. Until the late 1970s, in most primary school classrooms there was only one adult, supported by a remedial reading teacher who was shared by the whole school, and occasional parent volunteers. With the introduction of special educational needs laws in the early 1970s, large numbers of TAs began to be employed in special schools, where all children with special needs received their education in those early days of entitlement to education for all children. There were also a few LEAs such as the Inner London Education Authority (ILEA) which employed TAs to work in ordinary classrooms, to support teachers who had to cope with pupils from a wide variety of ethnic backgrounds. The roles of these early TAs tended to be of a housekeeping or clerical nature (cleaning paintbrushes, making copies, etc.) or in the case of those working with children with special needs, personal care or physical assistance.

With the move towards inclusion of children with special needs into ordinary classrooms and schools in the 1980s, staffing patterns had to change quite drastically, as TAs began to accompany pupils with special needs into ordinary classrooms, and class teachers shared pupils with special needs teachers. The TA who accompanied a pupil with special needs into the ordinary classroom was generally more knowledgeable about that pupil's needs than the class teacher. So it was often the TA who took charge of the daily learning activities for that pupil – a much more specialized role than housekeeping or hygiene. Despite these increased responsibilities, in the 1980s TAs were frequently referred to as 'non-teaching assistants'! However, LAs and the government have since recognized the more complex and demanding roles that TAs have taken on, and as we will discuss later, provisions have now been made to better prepare you for these roles.

Such is the nature of some TAs' responsibilities, it can be difficult to distinguish between teachers and TAs, and the question has been asked whether the Government is effectively replacing teachers with TAs, as a money-saving exercise.

Activity

If a friend or family were to say to you something along the lines of 'Well I think the government is just trying to save money by replacing teachers with TAs', how would you respond?

The reply to this question by the DfES was that TAs are intended to complement teachers, not replace them, and that the presence of suitably trained TAs in a school allows teachers to concentrate on the more technical and expert roles for which they are qualified. The TA can pick up those responsibilities which require lesser training and qualifications, giving a better match between qualifications and the demands of any given task.

Another question that has been asked in relation to the increasing numbers of TAs is whether this devalues the role of the teacher. The government response to this question is to reiterate the need for teachers to concentrate on the more technical aspects of their work, and for TAs to be suitably trained to support teachers by taking on the lesser responsibilities. Having two well-trained teaching members of staff in a classroom in no way detracts from the higher qualifications of the one over the other, particularly as one of those members of staff takes the lead and the lion's share of the responsibility. To quote the Education Regulations of 2004:

> Teachers are highly skilled professionals whose expertise and judgement are essential to effective teaching. They make the leading contribution to teaching and learning, reflecting their training and expertise. Accountability for the overall learning outcomes of a particular pupil will rest with that pupil's classroom/subject teacher.

Notice the reference to accountability here.

This is what distinguishes the professional teacher from the paraprofessional or TA – a much greater degree of responsibility and accountability. Although you must be held accountable as a TA for the tasks assigned to you, your supervising teacher is not only held accountable for the tasks he or she carries out, but also for those that have been delegated to you. Teachers and TAs are therefore not interchangeable, and no matter how highly qualified a TA may be, he or she remains a TA in terms of the level of accountability expected. At each level in the education system –

Activity

Take a moment to think about the different levels of accountability that teachers and TAs have, and write your thoughts. To what extent are you accountable for your work? And can a teacher really be held responsible for what you do?

----

class, school, education authority, government department – someone is held accountable for everything that happens at that level. The teacher is designated as the person held accountable for what happens at classroom level. As a TA you work under a teacher's direction and answer to the teacher, as he or she must answer to the headteacher for what you both do.

Appropriate roles and responsibilities for TAs

Four levels of responsibility

In the 2003 document 'School Support Staff: The Way Forward', the government distinguished four levels of TAs, according to qualifications, knowledge and skills, and the responsibilities they would therefore be able to undertake. At Levels 1 and 2 the requirements are designated as 'general' and are the same for all TAs, whatever their specific responsibilities. At Levels 3 and 4 a distinction is made between TAs working to support and deliver learning, and those providing behaviour guidance or support, a role which is most relevant to pupils with special needs. Table 1.2 compares the roles, qualifications and knowledge and skills considered appropriate for the four levels, for TAs working to support and deliver learning.

Table 1.2: Four levels of roles, qualifications, knowledge and skills required of TAs

Level	Level 1	Level 2	Level 3	Level 4
Basic role	To work under the direct instruction of teaching/senior staff, usually in the classroom with the teacher, to support access to learning for pupils and provide general support to the teacher in the management of pupils and the classroom.	To work under the instruction/guidance of teaching/senior staff to undertake work/care/support programmes, to enable access to learning for pupils and to assist the teacher in the management of pupils and the classroom. Work may be carried out in the classroom or outside the main teaching area.	To work under the guidance of teaching/senior staff and within an agreed system of supervision, to implement agreed work programmes with individuals/groups, in or out of the classroom. This could include those requiring detailed and specialist knowledge in particular areas and will involve assisting the teacher in the whole planning cycle and the management/preparation of resources. Staff may also supervise whole classes occasionally during the short-term absence of teachers. The primary focus will be to maintain good order and to keep pupils on task. Cover Supervisors will need to respond to questions and generally assist pupils to undertake set activities.	To complement the professional work of teachers by taking responsibility for agreed learning activities under an agreed system of supervision. This may involve planning, preparing and delivering learning activities for individuals/groups or short term for whole classes, and monitoring pupils and assessing, recording and reporting on pupils' achievement, progress and development. Responsible for the management and development of a specialist area within the school and/or management of other teaching assistants including allocation and monitoring of work, appraisal and training.

Level	Level 1	Level 2	Level 3	Level 4
Qualifications	Good numeracy/ literacy skills. Completion of DfES Teacher Assistant Induction Programme. Participation in development and training opportunities.	Good numeracy/ literacy skills. Completion of DfES Teacher Assistant Induction Programme. NVQ 2 for Teaching Assistants or equivalent qualifications or experience. Training in the relevant learning strategies e.g. literacy. Appropriate first aid training.	Very good numeracy/ literacy skills. NVQ 3 for Teaching Assistants or equivalent qualification or experience. Training in the relevant strategies e.g. literacy and/or in particular curriculum or learning area e.g. bi-lingual, sign language, dyslexia, ICT, maths, English, CACHE etc. Appropriate first aid training.	Excellent numeracy/ literacy skills – equivalent to NVQ Level 2 in English and Maths. Meet Higher Level Teaching Assistant standards or equivalent qualification or experience. Training in relevant learning strategies e.g. literacy. Specialist skills/training in curriculum or learning area e.g. bi-lingual sign language, ICT.
Knowledge & Skills	Appropriate knowledge of first aid. Ability to use basic technology – computer, video, photocopier. Ability to relate well to children and adults.	Effective use of ICT to support learning. Ability to use other technology equipment – video, photocopier. Understanding of relevant policies/codes of practice and awareness of relevant legislation.	Can use ICT effectively to support learning. Ability to use other technology equipment – video, photocopier. Full working knowledge of relevant policies/codes of practice and awareness of	Can use ICT effectively to support learning. Full working knowledge of relevant policies/codes of practice/legislation. Working knowledge and experience of national/foundation stage

21

Table 1.2: continued

Level	Level 1	Level 2	Level 3	Level 4
	Work constructively as part of a team, understanding classroom roles and responsibilities and your own position within these.	General understanding of national/foundation stage curriculum and other basic learning programmes/strategies. Basic understanding of child development and learning. Ability to self-evaluate learning needs and actively seek learning opportunities. Ability to relate well to children and adults. Ability to work constructively as part of a team, understanding classroom roles and responsibilities and your own position within these.	relevant legislation. Working knowledge of national/foundation stage curriculum and other relevant learning programmes/strategies. Understanding of principles of child development and learning processes. Ability to self-evaluate learning needs and actively seek learning opportunities Ability to relate well to children and adults. Ability to work constructively as part of a team, understanding classroom roles and responsibilities and your own position within these.	curriculum and other relevant learning programmes/strategies. Good understanding of child development and learning processes. Understanding of statutory frameworks relating to teaching. Constantly improving own practice/knowledge through self-evaluation and learning from others. Ability to relate well to children and adults. Ability to work constructively as part of a team, understanding classroom roles and responsibilities and your own position within these. Ability to organize, lead and motivate a team.

Activity

Which level of responsibility do you work at?

Take a good look at that level in the table opposite, to see how the description compares with what you do – your assigned roles, the qualifications you possess, and the knowledge and skills you are expected to have. Make a note here of any discrepancies you can see between what the government prescribes (in the table) and the realities of your current position.

Basic role:

Qualifications:

Knowledge and skills:

As you can see from the table, there is a gradual increase in the knowledge and skills required of TAs as the levels of responsibility increase. There is also a corresponding decrease of intensity in the supervision that is required from a professional. At Level 4, TAs can not only take on considerable responsibility for teaching but can also work quite independently, even supervising other TAs and monitoring their work.

Standards for your work as a TA

Earlier in the chapter we considered the differing levels of accountability assigned to teachers and TAs. A critical component of accountability is the presence of standards: benchmarks or expected levels of performance against which we can measure our own efforts. We will look at two sets of standards for TAs here: the National Occupational Standards, and the standards for Higher Level Teaching Assistants (HLTAs).

National Occupational Standards

The Training and Development Agency for Schools (TDA) is the government department responsible for standards of teaching in our schools. To ensure consistency across schools and LAs, National Occupational Standards have been produced for teachers, but also since 2002 for TAs – the National Occupational Standards for Teaching/Classroom Assistants. Other National Occupational Standards developed for education personnel include playworkers, early years workers and school administrators. National Occupational Standards (NOS) consist of a list of competences considered necessary for a person to be effective in a particular occupation, and the government recommends that the National Occupational Standards should be used for developing job descriptions, recruiting new staff and for staff appraisals. They provide benchmarks of good practice, and describe factors that contribute to effective performance. Details of the National Occupational Standards for TAs can be found through the Local Government Employers website (www.lge.gov.uk).

The basic ideas that underpin the Standards for TAs include:

1. working in partnership with the teacher;
2. working within statutory and organizational frameworks;
3. supporting inclusion;
4. equal opportunities;

5. anti-discrimination;
6. celebrating diversity;
7. promoting pupils' independence;
8. confidentiality;
9. continuous professional development.

At the end of the chapter you will find some suggestions on how you can apply these standards to what you do on a daily basis.

Professional standards for Higher Level Teaching Assistants (HLTAs)

The HLTA qualification, as you may have noticed from the earlier table comparing the different levels of TAs, is associated with the highest level, Level 4. The HLTA programme was conceived in response to concerns over teachers' workloads, and over who could provide classroom support at a level which would relieve teachers of some of their responsibilities while preserving teachers' status. In 2004, the government produced a document 'The Education (Specified Work and Registration) Regulations' which provided guidance on who could appropriately undertake 'specified work' – meaning, in this case, such tasks as preparing, planning and delivering lessons and assessing pupils' performance. Formerly these were only considered appropriate tasks for teachers. Essentially the document authorized schools to use TAs for this type of work, but preferably only those who had attained Higher Level status. It also listed professional standards for HLTAs, under three headings:

- Professional Values and Practice;
- Knowledge and Understanding;
- Teaching and Learning Activities.

Table 1.3 gives a summary of the areas covered under these headings.

Table 1.3: Professional standards for HLTAs

1. **Professional values and practice**
a. Have high expectations of all pupils; respect social, cultural, linguistic, religious and ethnic backgrounds; commit to raising educational achievement.
b. Build and maintain successful relationships with pupils; treat them consistently, with respect and consideration, and with concern for their development as learners.
c. Demonstrate and promote the positive values, attitudes and behaviour they expect from pupils.
d. Work collaboratively with colleagues, knowing when to seek help and advice.
e. Liaise sensitively and effectively with parents and carers.
f. Improve their own practice, through observation, evaluation and discussion with colleagues.

2. **Knowledge and understanding**
a. Have sufficient understanding of their specialist area to support pupils' learning; acquire further knowledge to contribute effectively and with confidence.
b. Be familiar with the school curriculum, age-related expectations of pupils, and the relevant teaching methods and testing/examination frameworks.
c. Understand the aims, content, teaching strategies and intended outcomes for lessons, and understand the place of these in the overall teaching programme.
d. Know how to use ICT to advance pupils' learning.
e. Know the key factors that affect the way pupils learn.
f. Have a qualification in English/literacy and mathematics/numeracy equivalent to at least Level 2 of the National Qualifications Framework.
g. Be aware of the statutory frameworks relevant to their role.
h. Know the legal definition of Special Educational Needs, familiar with the SEN Code of Practice, and know key factors that affect the way SEN pupils learn.
i. Know a range of strategies to promote good behaviour and establish a purposeful and disciplined learning environment.

3. Teaching and learning activities
a. Planning and expectations
    i. Contribute effectively to teachers' planning and preparation of lessons.
    ii. Within a framework set by the teacher, plan their role in lessons including how they will provide feedback to pupils and colleagues on pupil learning and behaviour.
    iii. Contribute effectively to the selection and preparation of teaching resources to meet the diversity of pupil needs and interests.
    iv. Contribute to planning opportunities for pupils to learn in out-of-school contexts, in accordance with school policies and procedures.
b. Monitoring and assessing
    i. Support teachers in evaluating pupil progress through a range of assessment activities.
    ii. Monitor pupil responses to learning tasks and modify their approach accordingly.
    iii. Monitor pupil participation and progress, providing feedback to teachers, and giving constructive support to pupils as they learn.
    iv. Contribute to maintaining and analysing records of pupil progress.
c. Teaching and learning activities
    i. Use clearly structured teaching and learning activities to interest and motivate pupils and advance learning.
    ii. Communicate effectively and sensitively with pupils.
    iii. Promote and support the inclusion of all pupils in learning activities.
    iv. Use behaviour management strategies, in line with the school's policy and procedures, which contribute to a purposeful learning environment.
    v. Advance pupil learning in a range of settings, including work with individuals, small groups and the whole class.
    vi. Guide the work of other adults supporting teaching and learning.
    vii. Recognize and respond effectively to equal opportunities issues, by challenging stereotyped views, bullying or harassment.
    viii. Organize and manage learning activities, physical teaching space and resources under their responsibility.

You will notice that the standards cover a very broad range of activities. You might almost imagine that they relate to a teacher's role. However, there is clear indication throughout Section 3: 'Teaching and Learning Activities' that HLTAs are still required to work *under the direction of a teacher*. And even in other sections, for example, in Item 2c (understand the aims, content, teaching strategies and intended outcomes for lessons, and understand the place of these in the overall teaching programme), the phrase 'in the overall teaching programme' suggests that HLTAs are not responsible for the overall programme, only parts of it.

Formal qualifications available to TAs in England and Wales

Since 2000 a variety of formal qualifications have become available to TAs. In this section we look at National Vocational Qualifications (NVQs), Modern Apprenticeships, the Higher Level Teaching Assistant qualification and Foundation Degrees. First, although this does not lead to a formal qualification, we look briefly at Induction Training for TAs, as it is a formal training programme required by the government, and it begins a programme of professional development which TAs are now expected to undertake and maintain throughout their professional career.

Induction training to support literacy and numeracy
All new TAs should undergo induction training of some sort – they should be introduced to the other members of staff (particularly those with whom they will be working), given a general orientation to the school buildings and timetable, and be given information on who they should go to for advice on different aspects of their work. This type of orientation should be carried out by someone in the school, and the school should also ensure that new employees have passed police and CRB checks, and are trained in health and safety issues.

Activity

Think back to when you first started working as a TA.
Did you receive induction training from your school or LA?

If you did, what topics or important points do you remember from the training?

How long did the training last?

If you did not receive any induction training when you started as a TA, have you been offered induction training in the last few years, since the government introduced the new induction training?

The government now requires LAs to administer an induction programme for new TAs – ideally four days of training, with a strong emphasis on supporting the national literacy and numeracy strategies from Reception to Year 6. The government has provided materials for the training (which you can read on the TDA website – address in the Appendix).The training is also considered appropriate for TAs working at secondary level, and in other subject areas, as the materials provided can be adapted to local needs, and expanded if necessary. There are four modules, covering:

1. the TA's role in supporting teaching and learning;
2. the National Literacy Strategy;
3. the National Numeracy Strategy;
4. how TAs can promote high standards of child behaviour.

Each TA should be assigned a mentor from within the school. The mentor should supervise activities undertaken by the TA during and after the induction training.

National Vocational Qualifications (NVQs)

National Vocational Qualifications (NVQs in England and Wales – or Scottish Vocational Qualifications (SVQs) in Scotland) were developed in response to the National Occupational Standards for TAs. NVQs are available at Levels 2 and 3, with mandatory and optional items at each level.

For NVQ Level 2 TAs must pass seven units of competence from the National Occupational Standards. Four are mandatory:

1. help with classroom resources and records;
2. help with care and support of pupils;
3. provide support for learning activities;
4. provide effective support for your colleagues.

Three more units can be chosen from the remaining five:

1. literacy/numeracy;
2. management of behaviour;
3. pupil safety and security,;
4. pupil health and well-being;
5. ICT.

At Level 3 of the NVQ, TAs must pass ten units of competence from the National Occupational Standards, four mandatory and six optional, although some credit can be carried forward from Level 2. The mandatory units are:

1. management of behaviour;
2. establishing and maintaining relationships with individuals and groups;
3. supporting pupils during learning activities;
4. reviewing and developing your own professional practice.

NVQs are work-based qualifications – that is, the TA must already be in employment, so that assignments and assessments can be based on current responsibilities and performance.

Modern Apprenticeships

A relatively new qualification that has been available to TAs since 2004, is the Modern Apprenticeship (often abbreviated to 'MA', but not to be confused with a Master of Arts, which is a postgraduate degree). Apprenticeships have been available for many years, but largely for young people aged 14 to 25. Like NVQs, apprenticeships are a form of work-based learning. They provide training through a combination of college courses and work experience, with government funding often available to cover tuition fees and a small weekly wage paid to the apprentice by the employer. The apprentice typically spends three days in training during the first year, and two days with the employer; this is reduced to one day of college during the second year. Many apprenticeships can be completed within two years. This combination of college and practical application on the job is intended to provide a high level technical qualification. Apprenticeships are always based on a partnership between a training organization (such as a college) and an employer in the appropriate industry, so that new knowledge can immediately be applied to a work situation. The college instruction is supplemented by on the job training, ideally from someone who is well qualified in the relevant skills.

Modern Apprenticeships use this same model of a partnership between a training organization and industry, as the apprentice must already be in employment in order to be accepted for the training. However, the modern apprenticeship is not a set course of study or a specific qualification, but rather a package of qualifications appropriate to the skills needed for the chosen career. So although the MA is typically made up of a combination of Key Skills, National Vocational Qualifications (NVQs) and a Technical certificate (such as a BTEC or

City and Guilds), those qualifications can be gained singly and independently. There is also a variety of ways in which some of the qualifications can be gained or demonstrated. For example, the Key Skills component can be satisfied by a GCSE or 'O' level in English or mathematics. So if a TA wishes to apply for a Modern Apprenticeship, and already has a GCSE in mathematics or English, there is no need for the TA to complete that component again – the GCSE can be counted as part of the MA.

Modern Apprenticeships are available at either Foundation or Advanced level. The Foundation MA is for TAs who have limited responsibilities, and who work under the close supervision of a teacher who plans the lessons and provides daily direction. The Advanced MA is for TAs who work under the direction of a teacher, but who contribute to planning, implementing and evaluating learning activities – in other words, those who have greater responsibilities and are able to work more independently. Table 1.4 shows the qualifications that are required for each one. There is also a Scottish MA, with some differences in the components because of the differences in the Scottish education system, but otherwise the qualification is essentially the same.

There is no fixed time period for the apprenticeship. When all of the outcomes are achieved, the apprenticeship finishes and a certificate is awarded, although certificates for the individual qualifications (such as NVQs) can be acquired along the way, and are valid even if the TA does not complete the apprenticeship. Typically, it should be possible to complete a Foundation Modern Apprenticeship in 12 to 15 months, and an Advanced Modern Apprenticeship in about two years.

Table 1.4: Qualifications required for Foundation and Advanced level Modern Apprenticeships

Foundation Modern Apprenticeship	Advanced Modern Apprenticeship
NVQ	**NVQ**
NVQ for Teaching Assistants Level 2	NVQ for Teaching Assistants Level 3
Key Skills	**Key Skills**
Communication　　　　　Level 2	Communication　　　　　Level 2
Application of Number　Level 1	Application of Number　Level 2
Information Technology　Level 1	Information Technology Level 2
	Working with Others　　Level 2
Technical certificate(s)	**Technical certificate(s)**
One of the following:	One of the following:
ABC Level 2 Certificate for Teaching Assistants	CACHE Level 3 Certificate for Teaching Assistants
CACHE Level 2 Certificate for Teaching Assistants	Edexcel Level 3 BTEC Certificate for Teaching Assistants
Edexcel Level 2 BTEC Certificate for Teaching Assistants	

Employment rights and responsibilities
Some aspects of Employment Rights and Responsibilities are covered by, and evidenced through, the NVQ and technical certificate. Aspects not covered must be addressed through an induction programme delivered by the employer and/or training provider. Evidence of induction programme outcomes will be internally verified by the provider and signed off by the candidate, provider and employer.

The Higher Level Teaching Assistant (HLTA)

The Higher Level Teaching Assistant programme came out of the National Agreement, Raising Standards and Tackling Workload, which was signed by government ministers, local authorities and unions in January 2003. The purpose of the programme was to recognize the high level of work that many TAs were already undertaking, and to provide TAs with opportunities to take on additional roles and responsibilities in order to reduce teachers' workloads. As with the Modern Apprenticeship, a TA must already be in employment in order to gain HLTA status, but unlike the apprenticeship the training component is quite minimal – a matter of hours only. The two major components of the HLTA programme are:

1. written evidence (in the form of a portfolio) that the TA meets the various standards established for HLTA status;
2. an assessment (through interview and observation) by an outside moderator or examiner.

As of February 2006, over 11,000 TAs had already achieved HLTA status, and another 4,000 were registered to take part in training, preparation and assessment.

In December 2004, the Teacher Development Agency commissioned an evaluation study of the first phase of the HLTA programme (April 2004–December 2005), to assess which aspects of the programme seemed to be working, and what changes might need to be made. The findings of the study were reported at some length, but some of the practical aspects of the findings may be of interest if you are considering HLTA status:

1. Teachers and headteachers were very influential in informing TAs about the training and encouraging them to take part, but TAs felt that school leaders should be better informed about the programme.
2. Application and registration for the programme were fairly straightforward.
3. There was a lack of consistency between training providers on entry requirements and the information and advice offered, as well as information on how to interpret and provide evidence for the standards.
4. All TAs reported an increase in their confidence, knowledge and skills on completion of the programme, including ICT skills.

5. Those who were able to work with a mentor found this extremely useful although it was difficult to find time to discuss their work with the mentor.
6. The majority of TAs thought that producing the portfolio was overly time consuming, although it was satisfying to map their work against the standards and see the extent of their role within schools.
7. TAs were frustrated by the length of time they had to wait for the results of their assessment.
8. TAs reported an increase in confidence and self-esteem because of the increased recognition of their role and the professional development (CPD) opportunities they were being offered. However they also felt that they should be given even broader recognition among the school workforce.
9. TAs particularly liked the HLTA pack developed by the TDA and made use of the examples provided.

The Foundation Degree for TAs

The Foundation Degree is another work-based training option that has recently become available to TAs. Because it is work-based, it is offered on a part-time basis, with some daytime sessions but mostly twilight sessions held in the evenings or after school hours. The courses are usually modular and cover topics such as learning theory, effective teaching strategies, behaviour management – essentially the same topics covered by the National Occupational Standards. Assignments for the course are related directly to the students' current classroom situation, and each TA must be assigned a mentor teacher at the school. A Foundation Degree typically takes 3 years to complete. One of the major advantages of a Foundation Degree is that it can usually be counted towards a full teaching qualification. There is a website listed in the Appendix where you can find out more information.

Chapter summary

In this chapter, you have considered how you would define a
TA, as well as looking at the government's definition. We have
also looked at how TAs fit into the education system, and why
we make the distinction between TAs and professional edu-
cators, based upon the differing levels of responsibility and
accountability. We then looked at the roles considered appropriate for TAs, with four levels of qualifications and knowledge and skills, as well as the National Occupational
Standards for TAs. A variety of formal qualifications have
arisen out of these standards, including the Higher Level
Teaching Assistant qualification, NVQs, Modern Apprenticeships and the Foundation Degree. All of these qualifications
can be seen as recognition of how your role as a TA has developed from early housekeeping and clerical tasks to being a
critical member of the teaching team, and the need for you to
increase your knowledge and skills accordingly.

How well am I doing? Self-evaluation exercise

This is an opportunity for you to consider where you currently
stand in your professional development, and the way in which
you might wish to move forward. As you can see from this
chapter, as a TA you now have several options available to you
for increasing your qualifications. First think about what qualifications you already have, using the list below.

My current level of qualifications is (list any formal qualifications
you hold):

1. --
2. --
3. --
4. --

Now take some time to check out options for further training and professional development, and consider which of them may be useful and available to you. You can conduct an Internet search, or make enquiries with your LA or local colleges. Don't forget to talk to other TAs as they may already have explored some of these options. Tick each qualification as you check it out, then make a brief note of what you learned about it, and whether you think it would be useful to you.

Qualification

NVQs

Modern Apprenticeships

HLTA status

Foundation Degree

2

Defining your role in the classroom

This chapter is where we take a good look at one of the two factors that will increase your success as a TA: knowing your roles and responsibilities. In this chapter we will look at:

- your job description;
- what your LA and school may have to say about the role of the TA;
- how your role is shaped by individual pupil needs.

We will then look at the details of your classroom role, especially as it relates to

- instruction;
- communication with parents;
- evaluation of pupil progress;
- behaviour management.

Lastly we will look at how you should clarify your responsibilities with your supervising teacher.

In this chapter you will find various words used in relation to your job description, the roles and duties you have in that job, and the responsibilities you assume. The term 'role' will most often be used in a general sense, for example, learning support or assisting the teacher. The words 'responsibilities' and 'duties' will be used for the more detailed aspects of your role: working one-to-one with a pupil with special needs, listening to children read, etc.

What is your job description?

When you applied for your current job as a TA, you may have heard of the vacancy through the grapevine, or you may have seen it advertised in the local press. Whichever is the case, you would have read or been given a brief description of some of the duties you might be expected to undertake. Typically, however, job descriptions used for initial employment are quite vague. In the box below there are two examples of vacancies advertised in the press for TAs.

Sample adverts for TA vacancies

Job Description
We need a Qualified Level One Teaching Assistant to work across all Key Stages. If you are enthusiastic and enjoy working as part of a team, we would like to hear from you. Telephone for details. Application forms from the City website or school. Please send SAE envelope. Interview date: 4th May.

Job Title: NNEB (+3)
Calling all Dynamic NNEB's and NVQ Level Threes! Are you available for immediate work? Do you want to be part of something special? We urgently require an experienced, fully qualified Nursery Nurse who can commit to a long term placement beginning after the Easter half term. You must hold an NNEB or NVQ Level Three qualification and have experience of working with early years children aged 3 years and over. This wonderful nursery school is excellently run and strives to maintain a positive environment for staff and pupils alike. We are looking to place a Nursery Nurse who is committed, dynamic and enthusiastic. Applications from any qualified and committed Nursery Nurses, who are able to use their initiative, would be welcomed. If you have an interest in this vacancy, then please submit your CV or call.

Look at the first example in the box. There are no details of the responsibilities you would be expected to undertake. The advert tells you more about what they want in the TA than what the TA will be expected to do. The second example does provide more detail, but again, you could only get a very general idea of what you would be doing on a daily basis from this advert. This is only reasonable when you consider the many different aspects of a TA's role – there are just too many details to list in the local newspaper – and, as we discuss later, each TA's role is defined primarily by the pupils he or she will be working with.

An advertised vacancy gives you an initial idea of what you might be doing. The next level at which your role becomes better defined is your job description. You should have a copy of your own job description, provided by your school or the Local Authority (LA).

▨ If you have it, take a look at it. Is it a good description of what you actually do on a daily basis? How much detail does it provide of what you should do? Have you taken on additional responsibilities since you began this job that are not listed on the original job description? Are there duties listed on your job description that you are not actually required to undertake?

▨ If you do not have a copy of your job description, it would be a good idea to get hold of one, as it will help you with some of the activities suggested later in the chapter. It also forms part of your contract with your employer, which is another good reason for making sure you have a copy. Talk to your teacher or professional supervisor and ask how you can get hold of a copy.

How is your role shaped by the LA and school?

As you read in the previous chapter, the government has provided guidelines on what TAs should be allowed to do, and what sort of responsibilities they can reasonably be expected to undertake. Your local authority (LA) may also have guidelines and advice on how schools in the area should use TAs. Much of this type of information should be available in your school or work setting, as LAs pass guidelines and policies on to schools and other education establishments. Copies of government guidelines are also often sent directly to schools. In addition, schools typically have a School Handbook, outlining policies and procedures that have been selected to meet local needs, and that have been approved by the school governors.

Several different types of guidelines are relevant to your work as a TA. These include:

- child protection procedures
- information relating to the Data Protection Act
- health and safety
- school discipline policies

If you have not recently seen copies of these guidelines, you should make a point of requesting to see them, as they provide general principles for the way you should work. They all contribute to creating a safe and healthy environment in which children can learn. As a member of the school staff, you are obliged to work within these guidelines. Although they may not provide details of what you do to support learning on a daily basis, they do prescribe general practices for you to follow, so that you also contribute to making your workplace safe and healthy for children and staff.

How is your role shaped by individual pupil needs?

The rationale for employing TAs in UK schools is based on the need for additional help for pupils. There has been some debate as to whether you are supporting the teacher or supporting the pupils – whether TA should stand for Teacher

Assistant rather than Teaching Assistant. TAs were previously known (and are sometimes still referred to) as Learning Support Assistants (LSAs) and this title really does describe the essence of the TA's role – supporting the learning process, generally by supporting individual pupils. While it is true that you are supporting the teacher in his or her responsibilities, your actual responsibilities are dictated by individual pupil requirements.

You may be employed to provide support to a specific pupil, perhaps one with special educational needs and an Individual Education Plan (IEP) or Individual Behavioural Plan (IBP). In this case, it is easy to see that your role is dictated directly by the pupil's needs, as stated on the IEP or IBP. You are there to help that pupil reach his or her educational or behavioural goals, and follow the plan that has been outlined to attain that end. If the IEP states that the pupil needs one on one tutoring in pre-number work or in developing social skills, then that becomes your role – there is a direct and obvious relationship between pupil needs and the role of the TA who supports the pupil. IEP goals and objectives give further details of the kind of support that is needed.

If you have been employed to assist in more general ways in a primary or secondary school classroom, the link between your role and individual pupil needs may be less obvious. But the link is still a direct one, as the classroom teacher assigns you particular tasks based on what he or she knows the pupils need. You may be asked to work with a group of pupils who need additional help, or your teacher may wish to work with that group, while you work with other pupils who can work fairly independently under your supervision. Whether you are assigned to the pupils who are struggling, or to pupils who are able and independent, your role is directly linked to their needs – general supervision as they work independently, or careful guidance if they are struggling with a task and need individual support.

The word 'need' is an interesting one. It suggests a lack of something. In an educational context, needs are usually based on a pupil's lack of ability in some area. For example, a girl in reception class may not be able to count beyond six, or may not understand one-to-one correspondence when counting. A boy in Year 8 may be unable to write fast enough to take notes in class. The shortfall, or what we might term a 'learner characteristic', creates the need for support. We will look more closely at your particular responsibilities in the next section of the chapter, but it might be useful to stop for a moment and consider the type of support that can be provided for pupils, and the extent to which it supports their learning rather than trying to make up the shortfall. In other words, whether what a TA does directly addresses the need, or whether it only disguises it.

In the case of the Year 8 pupil who cannot write notes fast enough, the TA's role may well be to take notes for him. Helping him to write faster is something that cannot be done during his history or geography class – he should get help for that elsewhere – so he is assigned a TA as a scribe to help him keep pace with the rest of the class on acquiring subject-based knowledge. In the case of the reception child who cannot count beyond six, the TA's role is obviously not to count for her, but to support her in the process of learning to count more ably. If the TA were to count for her and complete any counting exercises she has been assigned, she would remain unable to count. That type of support would only disguise her ongoing need, and confuse the teacher's assessment of the child's abilities and needs.

You will notice from just these two examples, that there are layers of need. The girl in the reception class needs to learn to count beyond six – that is a very basic need and a very basic skill. The boy in Year 8 needs to improve his note-taking skills (specifically his writing speed) so that he has something to refer back to when he is revising the material covered in class for exams, or to complete his homework. But he also needs to acquire subject-specific knowledge, and that really is the more basic and important need for him. He may never be a fast writer, but a good teacher would not want him to fall behind on knowledge acquisition just because his writing speed is poor. When a TA is assigned to support a pupil, the type of support the TA gives should address the most immediate and critical need for that pupil in that class or context. Needs have to be prioritized.

Let's apply this to your own working situation. Think of the children whom you support. Choose three of them, and fill in the 'Case Notes' form separately for each of them. If you only work with one pupil, think of three different needs that pupil has, and the different ways in which you provide support for each one. Where the form asks for a pupil ID, you should use initials rather than the child's full name, for reasons of confidentiality.

Your role as you understand it

At this point you should be able to clearly state your role – that is, the general duties that you have been assigned. In this section you will identify both the extent and limits of those duties. First some general remarks relating to:

- instructional roles;
- parents and the community;
- evaluation of pupil progress.

Instructional roles

Your title 'Teaching Assistant' assumes an instructional role. So we can assume that the larger part of your responsibilities relates to providing support for the teaching and learning process. For most TAs working in primary and secondary classrooms, this consists of what is sometimes referred to as 'guided practice' of new skills. The teacher presents new information or teaches new skills, then sets exercises or tasks so that pupils can practise those skills or apply the new information. This is

CASE NOTES
Meeting individual pupil needs

Pupil ID: ....
Learner characteristic that creates the need for my support:

Type of support I provide:

Pupil ID: ....
Learner characteristic that creates the need for my support:

Type of support I provide:

Pupil ID: ....
Learner characteristic that creates the need for my support:

Type of support I provide:

----

where you come in – working with individual pupils or small groups of pupils who need support to complete the exercises or tasks. They may need you to keep them focused on the task because of a short attention span, they may have difficulty reading the questions or instructions or writing their answers, or they may need someone to help them think through the problems or questions they have been set. In a secondary school setting where the volume of information and output is so much greater than in primary school, as in the example above they may need you to be a scribe and take notes as they dictate their ideas and answers. For a special needs pupil you may be helping them to manipulate or access learning materials. These are all aspects of instruction, so when you consider the details of your role, you need to take this into consideration.

Parents and the community
Many TAs would automatically dismiss this aspect of their role. 'Oh, I don't have anything to do with community activities, and of course the teacher deals with parents.' And largely, this is probably true. But this is also an area of particular sensitivity, which highlights your role as a paraprofessional rather than the professional. Formal interactions with parents – and especially reporting on pupils' progress – is one of the responsibilities that really belong exclusively to the teacher. However, this is not limited to parent–teacher conferences, or other formal meetings (such as IEP meetings for pupils with special needs). It also has to do with casual encounters between school staff and parents (or other family members) in and around the school or in the playground. Or in the local supermarket, or at a Saturday morning soccer practice. It is a question of confidentiality. From a legal point of view, the Data Protection Act of 1998 requires that any information about a pupil that is provided to the school will be held securely and only used for specific educational purposes. So when you consider your role as it relates to parents, family members and the larger

community, confidentiality and privacy are issues that you should bear in mind.

Evaluation of pupil progress

When you see the phrase 'evaluation of pupil progress', what comes to mind? Marking tests or taking exams? Or do you think in broader terms? Evaluation is obviously a general umbrella term covering many different forms of testing or assessment, both formal and informal. But the important question here is: to what extent is it your responsibility to evaluate pupils' progress? Let's take a quick look at some different forms of evaluation, so that you can answer this question as it relates to your own situation. The nearby box lists a number of them. Which of them do you have responsibility for?

Ways in which teachers check pupil progress and understanding

Exams (GCSEs, etc.)
End of term exams
Homework
Weekly spelling tests
Reports
Asking questions in class
Asking pupils to demonstrate a skill or procedure
Asking pupils to test each other
Watching facial expressions and body language
Observing how pupils react to an assignment

You probably have little or no responsibility for the first, most formal items in the box, but no doubt you frequently ask questions, or ask pupils to demonstrate a skill, because the responses you get tell you how much they understand. In short, you are evaluating their progress and understanding. And as a TA who works closely with individual pupils, you are often in a good position to assess understanding through facial expressions and body language. We have all seen pupils who refuse to make eye contact or become uncooperative when asked a question, because they do not know the answer. For your daily work this type of informal evaluation is as useful as exams and tests, because it is what is termed 'formative' evaluation: it provides you with information that helps you know what to do next in your teaching or learning support.

So, back to our question: is it your responsibility to evaluate pupil progress? Yes, because evaluation is part of good teaching, and therefore part of good learning support. You are constantly checking reactions and making judgements about what to do – and what to teach – next. Bear this in mind as you consider the specifics of your role in the next section of the chapter.

Formative evaluation

- Informal and frequent
- Tells you what a pupil knows
- Tells you what to do next

The extent and limits of your role

Although your job description may focus on a fairly specific role – for example, supporting literacy – you will most likely have broader responsibilities, even though they may be quite limited. So the question to ask yourself is: what is the extent of my role? This calls for a type of task analysis, which breaks down general categories and statements into more specific, practical, everyday terms: the sort of information which would answer the question 'So what exactly do you do all day?'

Imagine you are starring in a TV programme called *A Day in the Life of a TA.* Before starting to film, the programme presenter sits you down and asks you to walk her through your day so that she can get a better idea of locations and camera shots and the ways in which she can best portray the details of your working day. Your morning timetable may look something like this:

Time	Assigned role
9.10–9.30	General organization and help
9.30–10.10	Small group work
10.10–10.30	Work with individual pupils
10.30–10.45	BREAK
10.45–11.15	Listening to children read
11.15–12.00	PE
12.00	LUNCH

What the programme presenter needs is something much more detailed.

Use the blank form provided below to first make out a basic timetable for your daily activities. Then fill in the details of what those activities consist of. If your assigned tasks change significantly from day to day, choose the day you think is most representative of your work and that shows plenty of variety – we do want to keep the TV audience's attention! If you find that there are not enough time slots in the blank timetable for your working day, divide them up as necessary. If you already have a copy of your timetable and are keeping a loose leaf folder of papers relating to this book, you can use the copy you already have rather than the blank timetable form provided.

This may seem like a very minute level of detail, but it really is the level at which you need to know your role and understand the extent of your responsibilities.

The other aspect to being successful in carrying out your responsibilities is knowing the *limits* of your role: what you are

Details of my daily activities

Time slot	Assigned role	What I actually do

not expected to do. This may be in a legal sense, if government or local guidelines clearly state that TAs are not permitted to undertake particular work, such as selecting a reading scheme or modifying the curriculum for pupils with special needs. Or it may be more local than that, if your supervising teacher or headteacher has set additional limits on your responsibilities. Therefore as you complete the exercise on defining your role, bear in mind how much is required of you, but also where the line is drawn that limits your responsibilities. Consider this example.

Your new teacher has described your responsibilities to you and you feel that you understand what he wants, but then he adds, '. . . and otherwise, just make yourself generally useful'. You wonder what this means. His desk is very untidy – he'll surely never be able to find any papers that get left on it – so should you tidy it up for him? And now that you take a closer look, there's a general lack of organization in the room. It's just the sort of job you enjoy, but is that what he meant when he said you should make yourself useful? Would he be offended or pleased if you reorganized the room?

This is a fairly frivolous example of the confusion that can arise if a role is not clearly defined, and a TA risks overstepping his or her responsibilities. In this case, the worst that is likely to happen is that the TA causes mild offence by clearing up or tidying papers. But in the case of a TA who shares too much information with parents, or takes on more responsibility for correcting a child's behaviour than he or she should, the consequences can be much more serious than mild annoyance.

Use the left-hand column of the form below to list each of your general responsibilities, and then for each area fill in the column to the right. Re-read some of the previous sections of the chapter if you need a reminder about the areas listed on the form, or about the different ways in which you address pupil needs as a TA.

The extent and limits of my responsibilities

My instructional role

My duties include . . .	My duties do not include . . .

My role in relation to parents

My duties include . . .	My duties do not include . . .

My role in the evaluation of pupil progress

My duties include . . .	My duties do not include . . .

What about behaviour management?

A role that falls to everyone who deals with children, but which is often overlooked in role definitions, is behaviour management. When you were in school it may have been referred to as 'discipline', and your school may still have a discipline policy that relates to the consequences of different types of pupil behaviour, but the term 'behaviour management' is now in common use, meaning the everyday management of pupils' behaviour. Everyone who works with pupils uses behaviour management techniques. They may be very poor techniques, or they may be excellent. They may be deliberate and planned, or they may be spontaneous and almost natural. Whatever the case – poor, excellent, or somewhere in between, planned, spontaneous or a combination of both – whether you realize it or not, you use behaviour management on a regular basis throughout the day.

This book is not about behaviour management per se, so we do not have room to discuss particular techniques here, but as this is an unavoidable part of your role as a TA, a discussion of your responsibilities would not be complete without it. You must know which aspects of behaviour management belong only to the teacher, and which aspects you must attend to.

What is your supervisor's approach to behaviour management?

Your supervising teacher may have clearly outlined for you how he or she approaches behaviour management, and you may have a copy of the school discipline or behaviour management policy. So does this take care of behaviour management? Almost certainly not. Behaviour management happens on an individual basis, class by class and child by child, so we need to consider behaviour management at the daily, classroom level.

All classes have rules. They may be written down and on display somewhere in the classroom (this is more typical in primary schools than secondary schools), or they may have been explained to the class early on in the year, with reminders given when pupils seem to have forgotten them.

Activity

List here the rules that apply to your classroom. If you work in more than one classroom, focus on just one of the classrooms.

Class rules form the basis of behaviour management, as they state the teacher's expectation of pupil behaviour. Attached to each class rule there should be clear consequences – positive consequences that the teacher uses to promote good behaviour (keeping class rules), and negative consequences that the teacher uses to discourage pupils from breaking class rules (indulging in poor behaviour).

So let's look at the consequences that are associated with various behaviours in your classroom.

Activity

What privileges or rewards are available to the pupils you work with when they behave appropriately and follow school and class rules?

Activity

What punishments or loss of privileges are imposed on pupils in your class when they behave inappropriately or break school or class rules?

```
-----------------------------------------------------------------
-----------------------------------------------------------------
-----------------------------------------------------------------
-----------------------------------------------------------------
-----------------------------------------------------------------
```

You will need to refer back to your answers as you complete the activity in the next section of the chapter.

What are your responsibilities for behaviour management?

Earlier in the chapter, you considered the extent and limits of each of your responsibilities – what they do or do not require of you. Did you include behaviour management in that list? If you did not include it, this would be a good time to add it to your list of responsibilities. If you did include it, take some time to consider the questions below, and make sure that you have given it thorough consideration.

The form on p. 58 is designed specifically for behaviour management responsibilities, with sections to help you manage the details:

■ Promoting good behaviour or compliance with class rules. Is your role limited to quiet reminders to pupils of how they should behave, or do you have a part in providing positive consequences for good behaviour? What types of rewards are you empowered to provide for good behaviour? Only encouragement and appreciation? Or are you allowed to give pupils points or other rewards such as free time?

- Discouraging poor behaviour (breaking rules). What do you do if you see a child misbehave? Are you supposed to just give a warning look, or are you expected to be more proactive and intervene directly? Can you administer any sort of punishment or negative consequences for inappropriate behaviour? What types of poor behaviour do you have to refer to the teacher for intervention?

Notice that you are not asked whether these aspects of behaviour management are part of your responsibilities – they just are, because you work with children. You are being asked to clarify the extent to which they are your responsibility.

As an alternative to the form, you may find it more to your liking to use Figure 2.1: Mapping behaviour management responsibilities. The large central oval represents your behaviour management responsibilities. The smaller ovals surrounding it contain aspects of behaviour management. You have to decide which of the smaller ovals should be moved inside the larger oval, because they form part of your responsibilities, and which of them can be left outside the central area, because they are outside your sphere of responsibility. The small empty ovals are there for other aspects of behaviour management that have not been included, but that may occur to you.

Interestingly we even use behaviour management with adults. Take this example. Your supervising teacher likes to have written notes on the work you have covered with a particular pupil each week. On a Friday afternoon, if you do not have the notes to hand to her, she asks a lot of questions and takes notes herself, even though you need to leave. So you make a point of writing notes for her, because then she takes them from you, thanks you, and lets you leave straight away. She may have a few questions on Monday morning, but that works much better for you than hanging around on Friday afternoon.

There is a direct cause and effect relationship between your behaviour (writing notes for your teacher) and the consequence

My specific responsibilities in managing pupil behaviour

My responsibilities in relation to . . .	This includes . . .	This does NOT include . . .
Promoting good behaviour (compliance with class rules)		
Discouraging poor behaviour (breaking rules)		

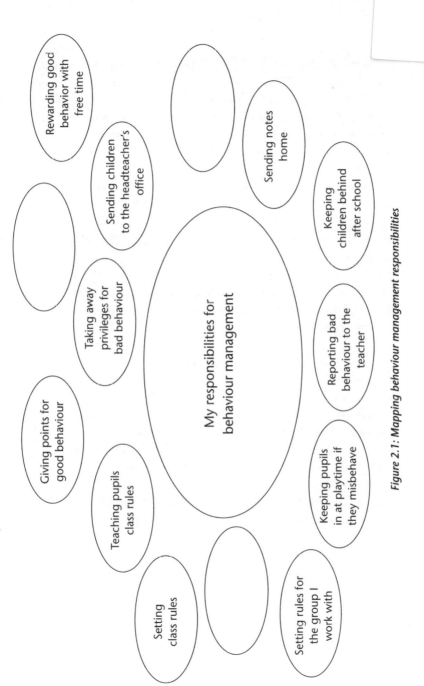

Figure 2.1: Mapping behaviour management responsibilities

of being able to leave on time. So in one sense, you are almost choosing your teacher's behaviour by your actions. Of course, you could say that she is modifying your behaviour: she gets you to write the notes by letting you leave once she has them. Is this behaviour management? Well, yes it is. And is there anything wrong with it? No, there certainly is nothing wrong with it. It really is all part of the give and take of working with other people – adults as well as children.

Remember, behaviour management is an automatic role for you as a TA, because you are dealing with personal interactions all day. It is also an important role because good behaviour management supports teaching. Pupils whose behaviour is well regulated – who understand class rules and the consequences of complying with or breaking them – are free to get on with their real work in the classroom, which is learning. And you are then also free to get on with your work of supporting that learning.

Using discretion in behaviour management

As part of your instructional role, you may be assigned to work with individual pupils or small groups. This may be in the classroom with your supervising teacher, or it may be in another adjoining room. Under these circumstances, it may well be appropriate for you to modify behavioural expectations and allow pupils to 'break' classroom rules.

An obvious example is the typical class rule that pupils must raise a hand to answer a question rather than shouting out an answer. If you were working with just one pupil, you would obviously not expect that pupil to raise his or her hand before answering. This may also hold good if you are working with a small group of pupils. Similarly, although the teacher may have some sort of points or rewards system in place for the whole class, you could establish your own system of rewards just for the time when you are working with your small group or with individual pupils.

Three considerations will help you decide whether or not you can modify a behavioural expectation or classroom rule:

1. *Will the change of behaviour cause disruption?*

   If you are working at a table in the same classroom as your teacher or other adults, and your students are constantly shouting out answers while the pupils working under the teacher's direction are working quietly, then obviously you must keep to the general rule of raising hands or giving some other signal for answers. Similarly if your small group of pupils cannot handle the change, causing disruption and disorder, you will need to use the more general classroom rule and ask them to raise their hands. But remember that disruptions are not confined to noise. If you add a system of rewards for your small group of children, those rewards should not disrupt the classroom system that the teacher has in place; they generally have to be rewards that you can offer and provide in the small group setting.

2. *Do your students understand that this change of expectation only applies to the times when they are working with you?*

   Children are generally capable of understanding that different rules can apply in different situations – they all know that granny will let them do things that mum won't! – but you should make it clear to them that the rule is being waived only because it is not necessary when they are working with you. They must revert to whole class rules when they are in the larger group situation. If you have children who cannot handle the apparent contradiction, you should keep to the class rules even when you are working with a small group.

3. *Will your supervising teacher approve the change?*

   If you wish to change a behavioural expectation for your individual or small group work, and have any doubts as to whether your supervising teacher will approve, you should check with him or her before making any changes. Your supervisor may know of good reasons why you should not introduce some of the changes, or may just prefer to keep consistency across the settings in which pupils work.

Take a moment to think about the different ways you modify class rules (or your teacher's expectations of pupil behaviour) when you work with individual pupils or a small group. In the left column of the table that follows, make a note of the class rule, and then in the right hand column, make a brief note about the modifications you have made or allowed.

Clarifying your role with your supervisor

Now that you have thought about your responsibilities, and clarified the extent and limits of those responsibilities in your own mind, the next important step is to check with your supervising teacher, to see if he or she agrees with your assessment. After all, it is all too easy to think you know what you should be doing, only to find that you have not quite understood when you ask the other person what it is that they want. This part of the process – checking your understanding of your responsibilities against your teacher's expectations – is important even if you have been working with this teacher for some time.

The easiest way to check your understanding with your supervising teacher may be to make a copy of your completed form, *The extent and limits of my responsibilities*, on p. 53. Ask your teacher to look over it and to let you know:

▪ Whether you have covered all aspects of each of the areas – instruction, parents and the community, and evaluating pupil progress (i.e. whether you have properly understood the extent of your role).
▪ Whether you have properly identified the aspects of the three areas that you do not have any responsibility for (i.e. whether you have understood the limits of your role).

Modifying classroom rules for small group work

Class rule/behavioural expectation	Modifications I make or allow
....	....
....	....
....	....
	....
	....
	....
....	....
....	....
....	....
	....
	....
	....
....	....
....	....
....	....
	....
	....
	....

The same applies to your analysis of your responsibilities in relation to behaviour management – show your teacher what you have written and ask for specific feedback on how well your analysis matches your teacher's expectations. You may find that this prompts quite a discussion between you and your supervisor, but this is all to the good. You are much more likely to work well together if you each understand what is expected.

It might be useful to mention a role that TAs often undertake and that has been somewhat controversial: covering for teachers. Government guidance states that support staff can cover for short-term teacher absences (when your teacher, for example, is off sick or attending training for the day). However, this is conditional on the TA in question being 'well trained and experienced', preferably with Higher Level Teaching Assistant status. And even so, that TA should be working under the direction and supervision of a teacher while providing the cover. It would be advisable to check local policy and procedures before agreeing to cover for a teacher if you are employed as a TA. You could ask your supervising teacher's advice about where you stand on this issue, should the headteacher ask you to provide cover.

Chapter summary

In this chapter, we have looked at some of the ways in which your individual role is defined and shaped. You have had an opportunity to consider:

- Your job description, and what you really thought you were taking on when you first applied to be a TA.
- What your LA and others have to say about the role of TAs in general.
- How your role is shaped by individual pupil needs, because ultimately – whatever your role – you are employed to provide support for pupils.

- The precise details of your classroom role, especially as it relates to supporting instruction, communicating with parents or other community members, evaluation of pupil progress, and finally behaviour management.

Lastly, we looked at the need for you to clarify your responsibilities with your supervising teacher, because your work takes place within his or her sphere of responsibility and influence, and you are essentially deputizing for, or acting on behalf of the teacher.

And therein lies the importance of understanding the details of your role. As you stand in place of the teacher, providing support for the learning process, you should not overstep the bounds of what is legally allowable, or instructionally defensible. You should only take on duties that have been assigned to you, and should have a clear sense of what those duties entail. Knowing what you are expected to do, and what you are not to do will increase your success as a TA.

You can use the self-evaluation exercise that follows to check where you currently stand in relation to the topics you have examined in this chapter.

How well am I doing? Self-evaluation exercise

Give yourself a rating for each of the statements that follow. At the end of the list of statements, note what you plan to do about the areas where you have given a rating of 'Not quite' or 'No', including a time scale for when you want to have addressed those areas completely.

	Completed?		
	Yes	Not quite	No
1. I have a copy of my job description from the school or LA.			
2. I have considered the needs of the pupils I work with, and understand why I help them in the ways I am assigned to.			
3. I have read the school handbook/ guidelines on: child protection, health and safety, the Data Protection Act, the school discipline policy.			
4. I have given a copy of the appropriate forms to my supervising teacher so that he or she can check whether we agree on the extent and limits of my responsibilities relating to: instruction, parents and community, evaluating pupil progress, behaviour management.			

I will complete the items marked 'Not quite' or 'No' by the follow-ing date: _____

3

Skills and assets required for your role

In the previous chapter, you considered the details of your various responsibilities in the areas of instruction, liaison with parents and the community, evaluating pupils' progress and behaviour management. All of these areas of responsibility suggest the need for certain skills and knowledge, which leads us to this chapter where we look at:

- the skills and knowledge you possess, whether these are formal qualifications or acquired through general life experience;
- the skills required of you in your various responsibilities;
- some simple steps you can take to increase your skills and knowledge.

We will also look at ways in which you can tackle difficulties that arise in relation to your work, especially those which relate to misunderstandings about your responsibilities and your preparation for them.

Assets you bring to your work

As a TA, you may have attended training specific to your work, and acquired qualifications stemming from that training. This type of role specific training is obviously designed to enable you to carry out your responsibilities more effectively. However, as an individual you also possess skills and knowledge gained from other aspects of your life –

personal assets which contribute directly to your work as a TA. Many of these are so well developed and spontaneous that you don't even think about them, particularly the basics of reading and writing, and the ability to communicate, or other skills that you use on a regular basis. In addition, there will be many other skills that you bring to your work, from formal training in other fields or from general life experiences.

Formal qualifications and skills

In a previous chapter, we looked at some of the formal qualifications that are now available to TAs and that are specific to the TA's roles and responsibilities. But there are many types of formal qualifications that may not be directly related to being a TA, but can still be an asset in your current work. Here are some of the different types of formal qualifications that you may have:

- A qualification awarded by a professional body, and based on a practical skill, such as first aid with the St John Ambulance, or a Swimming Teacher qualification from the Swimming Teachers' Association (STA).
- A vocational qualification, such as an NVQ or an apprenticeship, in an area other than education.
- A university degree, in an area other than education.
- A professional qualification in an area such as bookkeeping.

There are many ways in which these formal qualifications can make a direct contribution to your effectiveness as a TA, because general principles that you learn in one area often apply to other situations. Working in schools also involves so many different activities and topics that almost any knowledge acquired in another field can contribute in some way. But formal qualifications also say something about you as a person. Think of how potential employers would see you because of these qualifications. They would see that:

■ You are a person who can set your mind to doing something, and get it done.

■ You are a person who is willing and able to acquire new skills and knowledge.

The actual subject matter of the qualification may or may not relate to your responsibilities, but the fact that you have acquired formal qualification says a great deal about the type of person you are.

Life skills and experience

Now let's think about your life skills, and the experience you have gained outside the classroom. Whatever your age and stage in life, you have skills. Even if you have just left school and are working as a TA as your first full-time job, you have skills and assets that can be applied to your current responsibilities. If you have not been in school for many years, but have been bringing up a family, you have gained many skills by dealing with children, and also with adults and organizations such as doctors and clinics, teachers and schools. Why make a point of this? Well unfortunately, the phrase 'just a TA' is all too common, but quite unjustified. As we discussed in a previous chapter, schools and LAs must make distinctions between professionals and paraprofessionals (that is, TAs). Teachers must take more responsibility because they usually have higher qualifications and they have received specific training for their overall responsibilities. TAs generally have less formal training, and are expected to take less responsibility. However, as an individual you do bring experience and skills to your work. You may even have greater experience than your teacher. As you work under the direction of your teacher you make a very valuable contribution to the classroom.

Take time now to think about the skills and knowledge you have. You can use the form provided to make a list of these assets, or you may prefer to use the jigsaw illustration.

You will notice that the form asks for assets on the left-hand side and the context in which you acquired them on the right-hand side. You can start from either side. Think about the skills you feel you have, and then note how and when you think you acquired them; or make a note on the right-hand side of the different employment and other life experiences you have had, and note on the left what skills you gained from the experience. There are a couple of examples on the form to help you get started.

Don't forget things like opportunities you had at school (playing on a team, homework, just being at school), the Saturday job or paper round you may have had as a teenager, or volunteer hours in the community. And remember that skills can be:

- mechanical (good with a screwdriver or handy with a sewing machine);
- academic (good with numbers or words);
- social (find it easy to talk to people);
- creative (play the piano, or design a display);
- organizational (good at sorting things out and making things run more smoothly).

These can all be valuable assets in a school setting. You may want to write your list and then come back to it after a day or two, as you think of other skills and can add them to the list.

If you use the jigsaw illustration below to think about your assets, in each of the pieces write two or three of the qualities you bring to your work from previous experience and employment. You might use:

- head pieces to note mental or social skills;
- hand pieces to note your creative or mechanical skills;
- leg pieces to note your physical or organizational skills.

Skills and knowledge I possess	How and when I acquired the skills and knowledge
Example: I know how to work hard.	My mother made me wash dishes and help with housework from an early age!
Example: I know a lot about how machines work.	I've always liked to take things apart to see how they're put together, and I like to do my own basic car maintenance.

Figure 3.1: My personal assets

And don't forget that there are also qualities and values that you possess which are an integral part of who you are, such as honesty, kindness and tolerance. It may be harder to consider these, but think about your basic beliefs and philosophy, and see if you can identify when and how you gained these values. If you get stuck, think of some of the qualities you value in people you work with, or in members of your family, and ask yourself whether you have those qualities and where or how you learned them. While these qualities and values may not be listed on your job specifications, they do contribute to your keeping your job after you get it, and your being recommended for promotion or other professional opportunities. Consider two TAs, both of whom meet all the skill and training requirements for advancement, but one of whom is known to misrepresent the truth, or be unreliable. The well-trained TA who is also punctual, honest and fair will surely have the better prospects and be more valued by his or her employer.

What skills does your job require?

Now that you have thought about the skills and assets you possess, let's think about what your job responsibilities actually require of you. In this way you can start to look more closely at the match between your skills and the job requirements, rather than looking at your skills in a vacuum. In the previous chapter, you listed your assigned duties with details of what those duties do and do not include. Think back to these duties and consider them now in terms of the skills they require of you. For example, you may have listed 'listening to children read' as a duty, in which case let's assume that when you filled out the form you wrote something like this:

Instructional role: Listening to children read

My duties include . . .   *My duties do not include . . .*

Correcting words that are misread.   Reading to them.

Helping them sound out new
words.

Testing them on the vocabulary
at the end of the book.

Notice that all of the items listed are activities: something that you *do* in relation to listening to children read. Now think about the *skills* that are required for you to carry out the activities related to this responsibility. Here's an example of what you might write in relation to the skills needed for listening to children read:

Listening to children read

- Ability to listen and pay attention.

- Ability to read.

- Knowledge of phonics.

- Patience with those who struggle.

- ....

- ....

- ....

Notice here that some of the items on the list would be considered knowledge (phonics), some are practical skills (reading) and some are personal characteristics or traits (patience). Add any other skills that you can think of in the spaces.

Hopefully this simple analysis of your skills and duties has given you new insight into skills you already have, and the extent to which they match your job requirements. Most TAs who complete this type of activity find it rewarding to see how many skills they possess. Not only is it encouraging to realize how much you already know, but it also provides incentive to learn more. So in this next section we will look at some simple ways in which you can increase the breadth, depth and number of your skills.

Activity

Now think through your own job responsibilities. You probably have too many to analyse them all in this way, so choose about four, making sure you select a variety of duties which make different types of demands on you.

Duty:
Skills required:
•
•
•
•
Duty:
Skills required:
•
•
•
•
Duty:
Skills required:
•
•
•
•
Duty:
Skills required:
•
•
•
•

How to increase your skills and knowledge

In a previous chapter we discussed the various formal qualifications now available to TAs. However, you may not be able to access formal training for a variety of reasons which are outside your control:

- you may not have the time if it takes place outside work hours;
- you may not be able to afford the training, and there may be no funding available to support your study;
- you may live too far away from an institution of higher education or other establishment which offers the training.

Nevertheless, there are other ways of increasing your skills and knowledge, which are directly within your control. We will look at two of them here: enlisting the help of your supervisor to maximize learning opportunities; and taking on a personal programme of study and reading.

Enlisting the help of your supervisor to maximize learning opportunities

Working proactively with your supervising teacher is one of the very valuable ways in which you can increase your skills and knowledge. Rather than just working in the same space and with the same children as your teacher, you can take deliberate steps to improve your effectiveness through your daily associations. Being a TA can be like an ongoing apprenticeship. The Modern Apprenticeship requires a TA to be employed in a school setting, because the practical aspects of the job are so important to the learning process. Even if you are not engaged in a formal apprenticeship, when you are working alongside a qualified professional you can benefit from that close proximity to learn more of your 'trade'.

First, you can closely observe your supervising teacher. Become curious about the details of your teacher's approach to teaching and managing pupils' behaviour. Ask yourself why he or she does things in a particular way. Watch carefully and see if you can identify the things that your supervising teacher does to:

- get pupils' attention;
- encourage pupils to focus on their work and minimize distractions;
- promote active participation in lessons and activities.

Keep notes if that will help you to remember the specifics. As you identify the strategies your teacher uses, compare them with your own approach and consider ways in which you can use your supervising teacher's example. Then choose one strategy and try it out for a week. Don't try to change everything at once, just focus on one thing at a time, and observe the effects. In this way you can gradually build your repertoire of strategies and improve your skills. As a matter of courtesy, you might want to ask permission before observing your teacher. Make a point of asking if you can observe when your teacher is doing something that you are also assigned to do, so that you apply what you learn to your own work. Even ten minutes away from your work for careful observation will make a difference if you do it on a regular basis and learn from the observation. However, even if you are not conducting a formal observation, try to be more observant about what your teacher does, and put your observations to good use.

The other way in which you can benefit from your supervising teacher's help is by paying closer attention to advice or directions he or she gives you. For example, your teacher may say, 'When you work with Janine, get her to sit with her back to the rest of the class. She gets distracted so easily, it's better if she can't see what everyone else is doing.' This is such a simple piece of advice, and it may be something that you would think of doing yourself, but it does represent a very good general principle which can guide your work with other children: the principle of using physical arrangements to minimize distractions.

Activity

Take some time now to think of directions or advice that your supervising teacher has given you recently, which you could adopt for other situations. Make a note of them here. If you cannot think of any particular directions you have been given, look out for some over the coming weeks and make a note of them as they occur. Then take time to consider what general principles they represent, and plan to use at least one of those principles in your own work.

Specific advice or direction	General application
....	....
....	....
....	....
....	....
....	....
....	....
....	....
....	....

Both of these ways for learning from your supervising teacher's example – close observation and paying close attention to advice you are given so as to extract the general principles – are simple and available to you on a daily basis. They do not require large amounts of time or effort – they just require you to be a little more observant and thoughtful about the way you work – but they can help you to increase your skills and knowledge to a significant extent.

Taking on a personal programme of study and reading
The second way in which you can increase your skills and knowledge is to take on a programme of professional reading. There is an increasing number of books on the market written specifically for TAs. Fortunately they are usually reasonably priced, and are on topics relevant to TAs' roles, so you can choose the areas you are especially interested in, or the areas where you feel the need for more information. You might start with a book such as *A Handbook for Learning Support Assistants* (2003) which is published by David Fulton, written by Glenys Fox, an author who has been writing books for TAs for many years. Several other publishers have also come to recognize the importance of TAs, and the fact that you need and want to increase your skills. You will find some suggestions for publishers in the Appendix. If you conduct an Internet search for publishers and books for TAs, use a variety of descriptors or keywords such as Learning Support Assistant, LSA, Teaching Assistant, paraprofessional and paraeducator. Another good source of reading material for TAs is the *Learning Support* magazine (Brightday Publishing, London). Details are available on the website www.learningsupport.co.uk. You should also be able to find books in your local library on topics such as literacy and child development, as well as subject-specific information such as history or science. Books written for parents are also often useful because they provide plenty of practical advice as well as some of the background and theory of a topic. When you choose a topic for your reading, pay particular attention to

those areas in which you have responsibilities as a TA, and most especially to the areas where you feel you may need to increase your knowledge.

Whenever you are willing to reach out and take on a programme of study and gain information through reading, you are enhancing your knowledge, becoming a more valuable employee, and adding to your skills and effectiveness. Your reading programme does not need to be extensive, and you do not have to worry about remembering everything you read – no one will test you on it! Read for the pleasure of broadening your understanding and gaining small insights. Then just keep reading at a pace and in the directions that you find most interesting and compelling. As you continue to read on a particular topic, the principles and methods you read about will become more familiar, and you will be able to examine your own experience as a TA to find instances of those principles and methods put into practice.

Dealing with misconceptions or difficulties

No matter how well prepared you are, or feel you are, for your responsibilities, there are always times when difficulties arise in your work. This is almost inevitable when people work together, as few people have exactly the same perspective or expectations as their colleagues. The major types of difficulties between teachers and TAs tend to be disagreements over an educational concept or technique, and misunderstandings about your responsibilities. Whichever is the case, there are some problem-solving skills that you can use for dealing with the difficulties constructively and effectively:

- Keep an open mind, rather than automatically assuming that 'different' means 'wrong'. You are much more likely to learn from a situation if you come to it without too many preconceived ideas.
- Ask for clarification. If your teacher's ideas or expectations

are unclear to you, or if your actions appear to have upset him or her, ask if you can briefly discuss them.

- As a general rule the solution to a problem is closest to the source. If you have problems with a particular individual, talk to him or her rather than to someone else. Or, even closer to home, consider what you may be doing to contribute to the problem before you tackle what the other person should do.
- Consider what your teacher's working preferences are. Does your teacher pay attention to detail? Does he or she like things written down? Do punctuality and timetables seem important, or do flexibility and spontaneity take precedence over routines? Taking note of such things, and working with them, will help you communicate better and avoid unnecessary conflict.
- Place difficulties and differences in their proper context, to get a perspective on whether or not the differences will affect classroom activities and the way you work with your supervising teacher. For example, you may think differently about when pupils are ready to read, but if you are supporting pupils in a physical education lesson, your individual opinions about reading will not be an issue.

As a matter of professionalism and policy, you will generally be expected to defer to your supervising teacher's preferences, particularly in relation to educational methods. But as two adults, you should be able to discuss differences, and as a TA you certainly should seek clarification whenever there seems to be a misunderstanding. This is part of the learning process as well as being part of the professionalism that you should maintain in your work.

The last bullet point above referred to the relative magnitude of differences according to their context. Sometimes when you take time to evaluate the true magnitude or intensity of a problem, you realize that while it may be an irritant, it really is not critical. The Problem Evaluation and Solution Builder below is intended to help you work through such an evaluation when problems arise. Use it the next time you have a situation to deal with, and see if it helps clarify your thinking and response.

Problem evaluation and solution builder

What exactly is happening?
Write a brief description of the event that has been bothering you. Identify when and where it typically occurs and who is involved.

What is the real problem in this situation?
Write the problem again, but leave out the emotion, any value judgements or speculation. Whittle the situation down to crystallize the real issue.

Rate the magnitude of the problem.
Rate the problem on a scale of 1 (a minor irritant) to 10 (a serious problem that needs immediate and careful consideration).

RATING: (Circle one)   1   2   3   4   5   6   7   8   9   10

Does it require action?
According to how you rated the problem (1–10), decide
whether you need to do anything about it.

What possible solutions are there?
Think freely about possible solutions to the problem. List as
many as you can think of, regardless of whether you think they
are likely to happen.

What I can do to start solving the problem?
Until now, you may have seen the problem as something that
someone else needed to resolve, but now you need to identify
at least one thing that you can do to start improving the situation and eventually arrive at one of the solutions you have listed
above.

The following case study has been included to give you an opportunity to use the information you have gained in this chapter, and put it to practical use in a real life situation. The case study is in two parts. Read the first part and respond to it before moving on to the second. After the second part of the case study, you will find some feedback on the issues covered.

CASE STUDY
The right person for the job

Part I

There's a new reading initiative in my school. The reading scores weren't too bad last year, but we're all running out of ideas for the literacy hour, so the headteacher decided we should see what we could do to inject some new enthusiasm into it and into reading in general, for the staff and for the pupils. I was really pleased when the headteacher asked me to be on the committee. There are two of us TAs, along with teachers, one of the parent governors and the deputy head. I've done a lot with helping children read in the five years I've been in the school, and I think it's really important that children get the best possible start in reading, so I don't mind the extra time commitment involved.

We had our first committee meeting yesterday. We're all enthusiastic about the initiative and nobody had been press-ganged into being on the committee, so there was a real energy in the group. The committee chair has a great 'anything's possible' sort of attitude, so it got a bit wild as we were all making suggestions and thinking about the weird and wonderful ways we could promote reading. Nothing was considered too outrageous, and it was a really productive first meeting. By the end we'd generated a long list of things to investigate so we could bring back information to the next meeting.

We were all given assignments at the end, and I was a bit

disappointed with mine: typing up the chair's notes, making copies for everyone and making sure the room would be free for the next meeting. All necessary, but when I think back on all the activities and events I organized for cubs when my boys were younger . . . I really used to enjoy planning it all out, contacting people, and just dealing with all those fiddling little details that most people can't stand: the certificates, the food, the prizes . . . I wonder if I should say anything to Cheryl, the committee chair, or if I should just do as I'm told.

What would you advise this TA to do in this situation?

Part II
Well I decided I didn't really need to do anything. My sister's always telling me to leave something for other people to do, not think I have to do it all myself, or that I can do it better than anyone else! So, I typed up the notes, made the copies in time for everyone to have them as a reminder of their assignments

well before the next meeting and checked the room was available. But I thought I'd take my son's laptop along to the next meeting and make notes as we went along, then if Cheryl asked me to type up her notes I'd just have to supplement the ones I'd already taken.

So this week we had our second meeting. Still lots of enthusiasm, as everyone came with the information they'd been asked to find. A few disappointments when some of our best ideas started looking a bit impractical, but still plenty that looked really promising. There were a couple of little snags, though. Cheryl looked a bit askance at my son's laptop, and made a sarcastic remark about 'our self-appointed secretary taking notes', which I thought was a bit of a cheek, because she was the one who'd assigned me to type the notes from the first meeting. But it wasn't serious. I've known her long enough to know she doesn't mean anything by it, and the rest of the group laughed (with me) because they know what I'm like. So I can live with that. The real problem I had with the meeting was . . . how can I say this without sounding rude? Cheryl – the committee Chair – was the only one in the group who hadn't done her assignment, and didn't really seem to know how to go about it. She'd asked the school secretary to phone the secretaries of the people she needed to talk to, to find out when it would be convenient for her to phone them. And of course the secretary hadn't had the time. Besides, most of these people she needed to contact are the sort you just have to ring and keep ringing – at home in the evenings as much as during the day – and most of them don't have secretaries. I'm speaking from my own experience here – you just get to know the best ways of going about things if you do them often enough. She wasn't at all apologetic about not having completed her assignments. In fact it didn't seem to occur to her that she was the only one who hadn't, or that we couldn't move ahead on several things because she hadn't made the necessary phone calls.

So, the question is: should I offer to take over this organizational stuff? I've done it so often before and I really like doing it. What would you advise?

Feedback

There are many 'right' answers to the challenges described in this case study, as the different natures of the individuals involved in any situation tend to determine the best solutions. However, there are some general points which are worth considering:

■ The TA could have asked her teacher for advice on how to act. Teachers are most likely to know the appropriate protocol, and the individuals concerned, so they are usually well placed to give sound advice. Your teacher is your first port of call for advice on school matters – although it would be too heavy-handed to ask the teacher to intervene. The TA needs to take action herself, but she can do it in the light of the advice her teacher gives.

- The TA considers offering to take on a role where she represents the school (making phone calls on behalf of the reading committee). Provided the headteacher (or even the deputy headteacher who is on the committee) gives the go-ahead, there is no ethical reason why the TA should not represent the committee and make the calls. Her presence on the committee is a mark of respect for her abilities and potential contributions, and denotes trust in her judgement.

- The committee chair may not know anything about the TA's background, and therefore will not know that the TA has relevant experience and is willing to take on particular types of assignments. There is no reason why the TA should not offer such information as assignments are being made. During the first meeting of a group such as this, a wise chair might ask committee members to introduce themselves and briefly describe any relevant past experience, because some of them might feel uncomfortable offering the information without prompting. But if this does not happen, it would be appropriate for the TA to offer the information.

- There may still be some teachers who think of you and treat you as 'just a TA'. If you are unfortunate enough to work with one, you may just have to accept it and not let it affect your sense of your own worth and professionalism. Hopefully, as you prove your skills and knowledge their opinions will change.

Chapter summary

In this chapter, we have looked at the assets you bring to your current work as a TA – that is, the knowledge, skills and qualities you possess that you have acquired through a variety of experiences during your life. You have also considered the skills required of you by your different responsibilities, so that you can identify where there may be a gap between your current level of skill and the level you need for your work. We discussed some simple ways in which you can increase your repertoire of skills on a daily basis by taking up a personal programme of reading, and taking deliberate steps to learn from your teacher. We then considered some general problem-solving skills you can use to resolve misconceptions or difficulties, with the Problem Evaluation and Solution Builder to help you assess the severity of a problem and the course of action you can take to resolve the issues. If you finish the chapter with an enhanced sense of your worth as a TA and an enthusiasm for continuing the learning process, the chapter has fulfilled its purpose.

The self-evaluation exercise that concludes this chapter gives you an opportunity to look at your skills in the context of what your responsibilities require of you, to identify areas in which you feel that you need to develop more skill, and to consider how you might go about doing so.

How well am I doing? Self-evaluation Exercise

Now that you have looked at your job description, analysed the requirements of that job, assessed your own skills, and considered ways in which you can enhance your skills on the job, here is a chance to bring this all together, see how well you are doing, and decide what action you need to take to create greater harmony between the requirements of your job and the assets you bring to it. Use the form provided as a guide.

1. List one of your job responsibilities in the first row of the left-hand column.

2. Detail the skills which that responsibility requires of you (second column).

3. Make an honest assessment of whether you feel you have each of those skills (third column).

4. Where you have answered 'No', decide what you will do to change the situation and increase your skills in that particular area. Attach a target completion date as an incentive to get going.

Repeat this process for as many of your job responsibilities as you wish, but be realistic about how much new learning and study you can take on at one time – this will be a lifelong process, so you don't have to tackle it all in one day!

Job responsibility	Skills this responsibility requires of me	Do I have these skills? Yes/No	If no, what will I do about it?

4

Working with your supervisor

This chapter focuses on your role as a TA working with a professional supervisor and as part of a team. Supervision is a legal requirement for TAs, and the extent to which you are able to work effectively with your supervisor directly impacts your general effectiveness in the classroom. First you need to consider who your supervisor is, and whether you have more than one. Then we will look at:

- What we mean by supervision, and what it might look like on a daily basis.
- The importance of daily instructional supervision.
- How you can work more effectively with your supervisor.

At the end of the chapter, you will find a case study that gives you an opportunity to put what you have read into practice. You will also find an exercise that will help you decide what you can do to contribute to the effectiveness of your working relationship with your supervisor, because supervision should be an active, two-way process, not something that you passively submit to.

The legal requirement for supervision

The Department for Education and Skills (DfES) clearly states in every document relating to TAs that you must work under the direction, guidance, instruction or supervision of a qualified teacher or other member of staff. The National

Occupational Standards for Teaching Assistants, for example, state:

> It is the teacher whose curriculum and lesson planning and day-to-day direction set the framework within which teaching/classroom assistants work. The teaching/classroom assistant works under the direction of the teacher, whether in the whole class or on their own with an individual or a small group of pupils.

This statement also shows why you should be under a teacher's direction as a TA: you are working with the teacher on the curriculum goals he or she has selected and according to his or her lesson plans. Notice that this is true whether you and the teacher work together with the whole class, or whether you are working with groups or individuals. The level at which a TA is working (that is, the complexity of the tasks assigned to a TA) will largely determine the level of supervision. TAs who have been awarded Higher Level Teaching Assistant (HLTA) status, are allowed to carry out 'specified work' according to the Education (Specified Work and Registration) Regulations of 2004, which you read about in the first chapter. This includes planning and preparing lessons, delivering lessons, assessing and reporting on pupil progress – roles generally reserved for qualified teachers. However HLTAs are still required to work under an 'agreed system of management' – that is, under the supervision of a professional, because as the Regulations also state:

> Teachers are highly skilled professionals whose expertise and judgement is essential to effective teaching. They make the leading contribution to teaching and learning, reflecting their training and expertise. Accountability for the overall learning outcomes of a particular pupil will rest with that pupil's classroom/subject teacher.

HLTAs are allowed to take more initiative and work more independently because of their skills and experience, and they are therefore also supervised less closely, but supervision is still a legal requirement.

Who is your supervisor?

There are several levels of supervision within any school. The headteacher is responsible for everything that happens in the school. He or she must supervise all of the staff in some way, either directly or through a deputy headteacher or head of department. So the headteacher is your ultimate supervisor at school, but you may not be supervised directly by him or her. On a day-to-day basis, your work as a TA is usually supervised by a teacher. Your job description, in fact, may contain a statement such as the following:

Responsible to:
The class teacher on a day-to-day basis under the supervision and direction of the headteacher.

The next important question is: Do you have more than one supervisor? You will have more than one supervisor if:

- You work with pupils from more than one class, and therefore more than one teacher.
- You have been employed by the LA to work with a particular group of children (bilingual children, for example) in which case you may have a supervisor at the LA level as well as someone who oversees your daily work in school.
- You work with the special needs teacher or SENCO in an ordinary school, moving from one class to another to support a teenager or other pupil with special needs.

There are two aspects to this question of whether you have more than one supervisor. First, if you do have more than one supervisor, you will need to consider each of the aspects of supervision that we look at in this chapter in relation to each of your supervisors. Second, you must know who you are answerable to, and who is responsible for you at any point in your working day.

Think of this second point in terms of a fire drill. When a school has a fire drill, everyone in the school needs to know where to go and who to report to: teachers and children are told where to congregate, the registers are handed out so that teachers can check that all the children registered as being in school that day are with them and out of the 'burning' building, and no one is allowed back into the school until someone (usually the headteacher) has checked that everyone is accounted for. Where do you go as a TA when there is a fire drill? You go with the child or class you are working with at the time. So if you work with pupils from more than one class, according to the time of day that the fire drill occurs, you would find yourself in a different part of the yard or school field, with a different teacher/supervisor.

The fire drill is an emergency situation, and supervision is not only for emergencies, but it does help to identify who you answer to during your working day. That person also has supervisory responsibility for you while you are working in their classroom or with their pupils. You should be aware that if you are assigned to work in a secondary school supporting a student with an IEP as he or she goes to different classes, the subject teachers may not consider themselves to be your supervisor. And yet, as the professional with responsibility for everyone and everything that happens during that lesson period, they are also responsible for you and for the work you do.

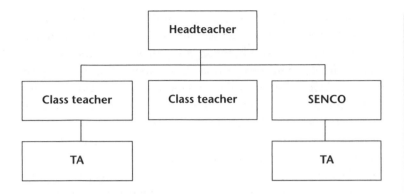

Figure 4.1: Typical lines of supervision in a primary school

Figure 4.1 shows a typical structure for supervision in a primary school, with a teacher or SENCO having primary responsibility for a TA, although one TA may work under both a SENCO and a class teacher. In secondary school, the lines of supervision are typically more complex, because of the size of the organization, and there may be several more layers (head of department, deputy headteacher, etc.) between the TA and the headteacher.

What is supervision?

So what do we mean by the term 'supervision'? What comes to your mind when you hear it? Is it:

- Someone looking after you, or looking over your shoulder?
- Someone keeping an eye on you, or keeping a look out for mistakes?
- Someone picking up on things you need help with, or picking on you?

It could be any of these, according to how you view supervision. And except for the last phrase – no true professional should ever 'pick on' a colleague – all of the other phrases really do describe supervision. Your supervisor is not only looking out for you, as your advocate and mentor, but also watching over what you do. Your supervisor keeps on eye on what you do, and also has to check for things you do wrong, so that they can be put right. This is part of a legal obligation to protect children under your joint care, and also to protect you. And of course, any proactive supervisor will be looking for things you need help with, rather than waiting until you come asking for help.

In the previous chapter on your role as a TA, we talked about the fact that when we describe a person's job, we often do it by describing what they do. Although this only gives an incomplete picture of the overall purpose of that job, it does give a good picture of what their day might look like. So what does a supervisor do? There are supervisors in all walks of life – in shops and factories and canteens. In fact there are many types of supervisors in schools. What does your supervisor do for you that you feel is beneficial, because it enables you to do your job better? If you feel that you lack supervision, what would you like to see a supervisor do for you?

Activity

Take a moment to list some of the things that you think effective supervisors do for TAs.

In simple terms, these are the things that a good supervisor will do for you:

- Watch
- Ask questions
- Answer questions
- Offer information

Notice that some of this may not seem very active. Watching, for example, may seem quite a passive way to supervise. But watching is a deliberate activity (as opposed to just seeing, which happens naturally through our sense of vision). And you watch your pupils, don't you? Why do you watch them? Make a note of some of the reasons in Figure 4.2 below.

Figure 4.2: Why I watch my pupils

You watch for signs of understanding or confusion as you teach, for signs of enjoyment or boredom, and for signs of appropriate or imminently inappropriate behaviour. Watching is part of effective teaching. If you are wary of being watched or having someone oversee your work, you are not alone. It can be quite unnerving to be observed as we work. At such times we feel our own inadequacies acutely, particularly if we feel that we are being judged or criticized. But in reality it is your supervisor's responsibility to judge your work in the sense that he or she sees what you do and assesses whether it promotes learning or not. If it does not, then he or she should correct you, showing you a better way of working. The correction should not be taken as criticism; it is a mirror of what you and your supervisor do for pupils as you try to adjust their behaviour and improve their understanding.

You also ask questions of your pupils. Why do you ask questions? In the speech bubbles of Figure 4.3 opposite make a note of some of the typical questions you ask your pupils, and then think why you ask these questions.

Activity

I ask these questions because

Figure 4.3: Questions I often ask my pupils

As a TA you ask questions so that you have information about what pupils know and understand, and so that you know what to do and teach next, or what you need to re-teach. You also answer their questions – a thousand of them every day! And you offer information. Does all of this make you a supervisor? Well yes, it does. You supervise your pupils' learning and behaviour. You monitor what they do and say, so that you can intervene when necessary and adapt to their learning needs. Is this why your supervisor watches you, and asks you questions, and answers your questions? In the same way, it is. Good supervisors do all of these things, because they are supervising your work, and that includes supervising your learning.

The box below also lists other ways in which your supervisor supports you and your work.

Other ways in which your supervisor can provide support

Your supervisor can:

- Help you learn about new regulations or guidelines for TAs, not only passing information on to you, but also helping you access training you may need in order to meet the regulations.
- Provide support and encouragement for you to attend training, finding out where you need to go, helping you study new material, and access resources.
- Advocate with the LA to help you get recognition for your qualifications and experience.
- Help you to access funding available for professional development.
- Ensure that you are performing your duties according to the regulations.
- Encourage you to document your training and qualifications so that you can build a portfolio or CV.
- Document training that he or she has provided for you in the course of your work together. If you are building a portfolio, this could take the form of a statement or letter identifying the skills you have been taught and demonstrated.
- Help organize efforts to lobby authorities such as lawmakers to support positive changes in regulations to employ, train and supervise TAs.

The importance of daily instructional supervision

The aim of the legal requirement for supervision is to safeguard pupils in the classroom and to preserve the role, status and overall responsibility of teachers in schools. This word 'safeguard' is not meant in the sense of keeping children out of physical danger (although that is something that you have to watch out for). Rather, it is a question of educational or instructional well-being. Children should be able to thrive as learners in the instructional environment that the teacher establishes for them.

In an earlier chapter we talked about TAs providing support:

- to pupils
- to the teacher
- to the curriculum
- to the school.

The first three of these emphasize your importance as a member of the instructional team within the school. A list of typical duties for TAs can be found in the box *Typical Duties for TAs*. Notice the words and phrases that are used to describe the duties that provide support for the teacher: assist, foster, work with, help implement. These are all suggestive of collaboration with your supervisor. The list of duties that provide support for pupils also emphasizes collaboration in an instructional role – to a large extent you are deputizing for the teacher. Thus the supervision you receive should relate directly to what you do to promote learning. Your supervisor must ensure the instructional well-being of the pupils in your care as you deputize for him or her, and assist in the teaching and learning process.

Supervision, then, is a legal requirement. It is also a very reasonable and logical requirement, given the important role you play in the learning process. But things that are required and logical are not always welcome. So let's think for a moment why you might want supervision.

Typical duties for TAs

Provide support to the teacher:

- free up the teacher to work with groups;
- supervise and assist small groups in activities set by teachers;
- foster participation of pupils in social and academic processes of school;
- work with outside agencies;
- provide feedback to teachers;
- help implement lesson plans;
- prepare classroom materials;
- implement behaviour management policies.

Provide support for pupil learning:

- develop pupils' social skills;
- spot early signs of bullying/disruptive behaviour;
- help inclusion of all children;
- keep children's attention directed to their work (on task);
- seek to enable pupils to become more independent learners;
- assist individuals in educational tasks;
- model good practice;
- assist pupils with physical needs;
- provide support for literacy and numeracy strategies.

Think of the analogy of parenting. What is it that good parents are trying to do for their child? Why do they supervise and take an active part in their upbringing? In the same way that parents help their children to develop skills and gain knowledge, to fend for themselves, keep themselves out of danger and work towards independence – in other words become responsible adults – so your supervising teacher is there to help keep you out of trouble/danger, and help you develop skills and independence as you become a responsible 'teacher'. You may not choose to attain the legal status of a teacher, but you can hone your teaching skills as a TA. Notice too the word 'good' in relation to parents and parenting. Some parents, fortunately the minority, are neglectful of their children and do not take active measures to ensure that they are physically or emotionally safe, or that they have the skills they need to be successful in various ways. In the same sense we can use the word 'good' in relation to teachers and other supervisors of TAs – they can be more or less diligent in attending to your needs, and in attending to their supervisory duties. In their defence it has to be said that most teachers have received no training at all in how to work effectively with a TA. Even newly trained teachers will have had little training in this area, and those who have been teaching for longest will have had the least in their initial training, and will be relying almost entirely on their years of experience to guide them.

Children are not always grateful for the supervision provided by their parents, but as an adult you can appreciate the benefits of having a good supervisor. Use the diagram that follows to complete the central sentence (I want to be supervised because . . .) in a variety of ways. If you run short of circles to fill, draw in some extras.

Working effectively under supervision

In 2000, the government produced a document entitled 'Supporting the Teaching Assistant: A good practice guide'. This document listed 12 things that schools can do to promote partnerships between teachers and TAs.

1. Differentiating the roles of teacher and Teaching Assistant.
2. Ensuring that Teaching Assistants participate in planning.

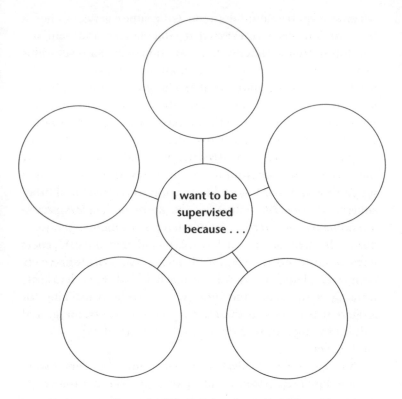

Figure 4.4: Why I want to be supervised

3. Creating a climate that encourages high quality Teaching Assistant input.
4. Developing feedback mechanisms.
5. Dealing with behaviour management issues under teacher guidance.
6. Ensuring Teaching Assistants are informed of the learning needs and any behavioural difficulties of children with SEN.
7. Including Teaching Assistants in IEP reviews.
8. Inviting Teaching Assistants to staff meetings.

9. Including Teaching Assistants in the staffroom.
10. Including Teaching Assistants in written communications.
11. Recognizing the legal responsibilities of Teaching Assistants.
12. Encouraging reviews of the classroom relationship.

Although these are very definitely recommendations for teachers and headteachers, you can take them as a basis for contributing to being an effective team member with your supervisor. Some areas may be entirely out of your control – such as points 8 and 9 – but there is usually something you can do to show your willingness and interest in participating in different ways, even if you do not have the ultimate decision-making power. At the end of the chapter you will find a self-evaluation exercise that uses this list as a basis for making your own plans for working under your supervisor. Meanwhile, here are some suggestions as to what you might do. Some of them will sound familiar, as we have already discussed them in earlier chapters.

- You should have a clear job description and understanding of your responsibilities. If you do not have a job description, ask for one, and take the time to ask your supervisor for clarification on the extent and limits of your responsibilities.
- Try to make yourself available to meet with your supervisor when he or she asks. This should be during your contracted work hours – you should not have to stay on after school without being paid – but time can usually be found when the class is working independently and only needs minimal supervision.
- If your supervisor doesn't ask you to meet with him or her for planning time, you can try and prompt this by simply asking whether he or she generally does that. This is especially easy when you start to work with a new teacher.
- Good communications are a vital part of making the

supervision process work for both you and your supervisor. You already know that pupils can try to play one adult off against the other. Good communication among the adults can prevent this from happening. Conversely, when communications are not good expectations may be unclear, causing pupils to be confused about classroom procedures and learning.

■ If you work with other TAs, check what their roles and expectations are, so if there is a difference of understanding or an overlap in roles, you can clarify expectations early on and avoid later clashes or misunderstandings. It may be possible to keep a folder with job descriptions or other information relating to each person's assignments in easy reach so that you can remind yourself of who is doing what, without interrupting other people's work.

■ Be supportive of all other adults you work with, especially in front of pupils. If you disagree or want to discuss a policy or procedure, make sure you do it later and in private.

■ Be an active learner. Ask questions and seek feedback. Watch for the good and effective things that your teacher does, so that you can incorporate them into your repertoire of teaching skills. If you do not understand why he or she does a particular thing, ask.

■ You may want to ask your teacher if you can observe him or her at work on a regular basis, discussing first which aspect of instruction or behaviour management you could focus your attention on, and afterwards discussing what you saw and the conclusions that can be drawn from your observations. This is apprenticeship at its best, representing daily efforts toward staff development and classroom improvement.

■ Respect your supervisor's preferences. There are usually many good ways of doing a particular job, but if your supervisor has a preference for a particular method or materials, and you know of no reason why they should not be used, use them, even if they would not be your first choice.

- Be well informed on school policies and procedures. Ask for information if you feel you need it.
- If you work with other teachers and have difficulties with anything that they ask you to do, ask your primary supervisor for advice.

These are just some of the many ways in which you can be proactive in contributing to the effectiveness of your work with your supervisor.

This last section consists of a case study relating to the issues we have been discussing. Read Part 1 and respond to it before reading Part 2; likewise respond to Part 2 before reading Part 3. Don't give in to the temptation to find out what happens at the end before you have commented on the beginning, even if you do that with novels!

CASE STUDY
Who's in charge here anyway?

Part 1

I'm a new teacher in this school. I worked in another school for 3 years after graduating, but moved here because I thought it was time for a change. And I'm glad I did. I like this school, but one of the changes that I hadn't anticipated was Pauline. She's my TA. I didn't have one in the last school, but I'm always happy to have extra help, and if I'm honest about it, Pauline's a real gem, very hard working and knowledgeable. When she told me when she started working as a TA, I didn't tell her that was the year I started junior school, but I suspect she worked that out for herself. And my only real complaint is that she does treat me like one of the children sometimes – not unkindly, but as if she

Working with your supervisor

109

knows best. It's nothing big, but there are times when she questions my decisions and interprets what I ask her to do rather liberally. She doesn't quite do what I ask her to, and she'll often point out how she's essentially improved on what I suggested. And I did overhear her talking to one of the other TAs, and telling them how much more she knows about children and classrooms than I do.

So what do you think I should do about it? Should I just ignore it and hope it all settles down? Or should I step in straight away in case it gets any worse?

Part 2

Well I did ignore it. I didn't want to be too heavy handed – especially as there wasn't anything wrong with what Pauline was doing, and I was more interested in getting to know the children better, and getting more used to the ways of the school. But we've been together for several weeks now, and I've had more time to think about it. I'd just about decided that it really was a bit childish to object to Pauline improving on my ideas, when I came in this morning to find that the classroom was rearranged! The tables and chairs had all been moved, and anything else that was moveable – the cupboards and tray units, the whiteboard, almost everything. I assumed the cleaner had done it – I couldn't imagine why – and made a mental note to talk to her after school. I didn't even think it could have been Pauline, and we were so busy today that we didn't have time to chat about anything except essentials. So when I mentioned it to another teacher in the staffroom during break, I was stunned to hear that she not only knew about my new room arrangement, but she knew Pauline had done it. She laughed when I told her, because her TA had already suggested they move their furniture into the same sort of arrangement. I surely shouldn't have to put up with this. I feel as if I'm no longer in charge – and the whole school knows it.

I really don't want a confrontation with Pauline, but I can't just let it be. So what should I do about it? What can I say to her that won't sound like criticism?

Part 3

Well the situation really came to a head this afternoon, and I can't avoid doing something about it now. I didn't have time to talk to Pauline about the furniture that day, and yesterday she wasn't in school (she only works four days a week). But today I needed Pauline to work with a small group of children who were finishing off a model roman villa they were making as part of our history project. They'd finished their writing so I thought they could work quietly enough not to disturb the others with a bit of supervision. I thought she'd like to do that, because she is very good with her hands – she's very creative, and she doesn't take over with the children in the same way that she tries to do with me. She gives guidance but let's them learn from their mistakes and doesn't do everything for them, even for the ones who will wheedle you into it if they can.

So I approached Pauline – who as usual was busy (she's no time waster) working on the display we'd agreed she'd take charge of – and asked her would she mind. I was apologetic about interrupting her, knowing she doesn't like short notice, but I was quite speechless when she turned me down flat and said, no, she couldn't help, she was busy with the display. And that was it. No excuses. No apologies. Just a flat refusal. I didn't have time to remonstrate with her – I had the class to see to – and her day finishes just before home-time so I couldn't speak to her once the children had left. This has really got out of hand. Do you think it's possible to get things back on to the right footing now? And how can it be done?

Feedback

In the first part of the case study the new teacher describes Pauline as 'a gem' but is uncomfortable with the extent to which Pauline is taking liberties with her instructions and ideas, and has pointed out their different levels of experience to another TA. It is unprofessional of Pauline to discuss her teacher with another TA, and to suggest that she knows more than the teacher, although we do not know how tactful she was in expressing those thoughts. But she may well feel that she is only doing her job in carrying out the teacher's instructions (and going the extra mile where she can see that they can be carried out more fully). Perhaps her previous supervising teacher encouraged this type of initiative. The new teacher is probably a little sensitive to the differences in their experience (and Pauline is probably quite a lot older, which can also be intimidating for a new teacher). So on the whole, the situation is not too serious, though the teacher should consider having a meeting with Pauline as soon as possible to express her expectations and allow Pauline to ask questions about her role.

In the second part, things escalate as Pauline takes the liberty of rearranging the classroom without the teacher's prior approval. We don't know why she has done it: presumably she thought it a good idea. But good ideas should be offered or suggested to your supervisor unless you know him or her well enough to do something as a surprise. Not everyone likes surprises, after all, and not all surprises are pleasant. The teacher should obviously do something at this point – whether she likes the new classroom arrangement or not – otherwise Pauline would be quite justified in thinking that she can make changes without consulting the teacher at all. Even if she doesn't have time to meet Pauline straight away, she should tell Pauline that they'll be having a planning meeting – during the working day, of course – and name a time when the class can work with minimal supervision. If she feels that this arrangement would be too public, then she should find an alternative time when they can speak privately and without interruptions, which may be best in the light of the present discussions.

The third instance of Pauline's behaviour that concerns the teacher is her refusal to change what she is doing and supervise a small group of pupils so that they work quietly on a project. This is not an unreasonable request on the part of the teacher, and all TAs should be prepared to adjust their plans at short notice – school life demands it of everyone. So the teacher obviously cannot go on ignoring Pauline's behaviour – which is becoming increasingly inappropriate – and must meet with her to clarify expectations. The teacher's particular concern about not criticizing Pauline is a common one, but her objections can be stated in positive and unemotional terms, rather than as a personal attack. And they could include an apology for not having made things clear upfront, which would redress the balance of the relationship. The teacher may have been able to avoid some of this type of behaviour on Pauline's part if she had taken the time to meet with her straight away rather than waiting to see how things settled on their own.

And what about Pauline? As a TA, what recommendations would you have for her in light of our discussions about working with your supervisor?

Activity

List the three most important things that you think Pauline should do to work more effectively under the direction of her supervising teacher.

Chapter summary

In this chapter, we have been looking at how you can work more effectively under supervision. First we looked at the legal requirement for supervision of TAs, then at the need to identify who your supervisor is, and indeed, whether you have more than one, which many TAs do. We then considered what supervision might look like on a daily basis, as well as the importance of instructional supervision, as your basic function is to support the teaching and learning process. Lastly, we considered some ways in which you can enhance your relationship with your supervisor, with the case study that you have just completed giving you an opportunity to apply the main points of the chapter.

Supervision should be one of the everyday realities of your work. You can promote active supervision, and show a willingness to work under the direction of your supervisor as you adopt his or her methods, seek feedback on your own work, and communicate your own needs and those of your pupils. The self-evaluation exercise that follows will help you plan exactly what you will do in these areas.

How well am I doing? Self-evaluation exercise

Earlier in the chapter we listed the government's recommendations for supporting TAs as they work with teachers. That list is repeated here with space for you to consider what you can do to contribute to being an effective team member with your supervisor. Areas such as being included in the staffroom and staff meetings (points 8 and 9) are almost entirely out of your control, but there are many ways in which you can contribute to the other areas listed. Use this list to generate specific things that you intend to do to work more effectively with your supervisor, rather than making it a list of all things that TAs could do in any situation.

Government recommendations	Critical elements	What I intend to do to promote these recommendations in my own situation
1. Differentiating the roles of teacher and TA.	Both teacher and TA need to be aware of their different functions.	
2. Ensuring TA participation in planning.	Good planning and preparation with clear objectives.	
3. Creating a climate that encourages high quality TA input.	TA confidence grows with time and comes from a mutually supportive relationship.	
4. Developing feedback mechanisms.	Feedback to the teacher by the TA, as well as feedback from the teacher.	
5. Dealing with behaviour management issues under teacher guidance.	The TA needs to be familiar with the school's behaviour management policy.	

Government recommendations	Critical elements	What I intend to do to promote these recommendations in my own situation
6. Ensuring TAs know learning needs/behavioural difficulties of children with SEN.	(Largely for TAs working with children with SEN, but also for those working in inclusive classrooms.)	
7. Including TAs in IEP reviews.	(Largely for TAs working with children with SEN, but also for those working in inclusive classrooms.)	
8. Inviting TAs to staff meetings.	(Out of your control as a TA.)	
9. Including TAs in the staffroom.	(Out of your control as a TA.)	
10. Including TAs in written communications.	Public acknowledgement of the value of TAs.	

Government recommendations	Critical elements	What I intend to do to promote these recommendations in my own situation
11. Recognizing the legal responsibilities of TAs.	Health and safety, child protection and other legislation.	
12. Encouraging reviews of the classroom relationship.		

5

Conclusion

Success as a TA

Well, you have almost reached the end of the book and you should by now have gained some useful insights into how you can be more successful and effective in your work as a Teaching Assistant. Let's just take a look at the areas that we have covered so far.

The story so far

In the Introduction, we looked at the need for a book such as this, as part of your continuing professional development as a TA. Whether you are engaged in a formal course of study or not, there are many ways in which you can increase your skills and knowledge, and a book such as this one can give you a good start. We looked at some of the various titles given to TAs, currently and in the past. We also looked at some facts about TAs in the UK and elsewhere – the USA, Canada and Australia in particular – and found many similarities, but also some differences resulting from differences in local needs and legislation. Then we considered some of the advantages and disadvantages of being an adult learner. Hopefully, by this point you will have decided that there are more advantages than disadvantages, and you will feel rather more confident and clear about your position as a TA, and about your ability to increase your skills and knowledge.

In the first chapter, we looked for answers to the question: What is a TA? Official government sources help to identify who TAs are and where you fit into the educational system. One of the most important aspects of being a TA, reiterated in every government source, is the stipulation that TAs work under the direction of a qualified professional. In the overall structure of the education system, this places you very firmly at that critical point of daily contact between teacher and learner, where you can have the most individual and meaningful impact, working alongside the teacher. We discussed the fact that the distinction between professional and paraprofessional reflects levels of qualification and degrees of responsibility, however, there are also distinctions made between TAs in terms of qualifications and responsibility, Higher Level Teaching Assistant (HLTA) status is considered the most advanced, bringing with it the opportunity for the greatest level of independence. We considered some of the formal qualifications that are now available to TAs in the UK – including Modern Apprenticeships, NVQs and Foundation Degrees – and the standards that accompany them, specifically the National Occupational Standards (NOS) for Teaching Assistants and the standards set for HLTAs.

Take a moment to think about your position as a TA in the education system. In the space provided opposite, draw a diagram of where you see yourself amongst other education professionals. Your diagram could take the form of a picture or illustration, or it may be a more formal version, but it should show where you see your place in the teaching and learning process.

In the second chapter, we looked at different levels at which your role as a TA is defined:

- in keeping with LA policy;
- in accordance with your job description;
- as dictated by individual pupil needs.

This sequence produces an increasingly well-defined role description, from general principles and procedures to specific

Your diagram . . .

duties and expectations. Once you reach the classroom level of definition, there are still many details which need to be discussed and settled with your supervising teacher:

- what role you will play in relation to instruction;
- the nature of your interactions with parents and the community;
- the extent to which you will be involved in the evaluation of pupil progress;
- your contribution to managing pupil behaviour.

This last area is common to all those who work in schools, although it is sometimes forgotten when responsibilities are assigned. We ignore behaviour, bad or good, at our own peril, because how we react to behaviour has a direct affect on our relationships with our pupils (and therefore on our ability to interact effectively with them in the learning process). In this chapter, you took some time to consider your supervising teacher's approach to behaviour management, how that approach blends into your role in managing behaviour, and the extent to which you can safely modify class rules and procedures when you are working with individual pupils or small groups.

Activity

Take a moment to think back on this chapter relating to your role and identify one or two concepts or ideas that seemed particularly important to you. Make a note of them here.

In Chapter 3, 'Skills and assets required for your role', we looked at the personal and professional assets which you bring to your work as a TA, and how those assets may or may not match with the skills your role requires of you. Your assets include not only formal qualifications and skills, but also life skills and experience. Where your current skills do not match the demands of your responsibilities, this signals the need for additional training to bridge the gap. You read and thought about the various ways in which you can increase your skills and knowledge, including enlisting the help of your supervisor, and taking on a personal programme of study and reading. Your supervising teacher is not only assigned to you to satisfy a legal requirement, but is also a very valuable source of professional knowledge and guidance. You can learn a great deal from observing teachers, but even more from discussing your joint responsibility for teaching and learning. And lastly in this chapter we looked briefly at some ways in which you can use problem-solving skills to deal with misconceptions or difficulties over your role. The chapter ended with a case study exploring some of the concepts in a real-life situation.

Activity

Take a moment to think back on this chapter, and make a note here of what struck you as particularly important and relevant to your own situation. Did you discover anything new about yourself? What new perspectives did it provide for your work?

The next chapter, 'Working with your supervisor', began by exploring what the term 'supervision' might mean. What do good supervisors do? And who exactly is your supervisor? You may have more than one, especially if you work with pupils with special needs, or in more than one classroom. This can complicate life quite considerably, but provided you are clear about what each one expects, you should be able to work effectively with any number of different supervisors. There is of course a legal requirement for supervision – quite justifiably, given your employment as a TA rather than a qualified teacher. But we also looked at the importance of *instructional* supervision – that is, the need for your work, which is delegated to you by your supervisor, to be monitored for effectiveness. Not as a fault-finding exercise, but to ensure that pupils are getting a fair deal, and are not being short-changed because they are being taught by a TA rather than a teacher. You were given the opportunity to identify some of the many ways in which you can be proactive in developing your working relationship with your supervisor, and the chapter finished with another case study, dealing with the difficulties that new teachers can face when they work with very experienced TAs. In this particular case, the TA in question seemed unwilling to accept supervision, particularly from a younger, less experienced teacher.

Activity

Make a note here of what you feel is the most important thing that your supervisor does for you. Consider both the instructional guidance he or she provides and the mentoring and advocacy that your supervisor undertakes on your behalf.

Activity

You probably already have a good working relationship with your supervisor, but make a note of one thing that you feel you could do towards improving that relationship, in light of what you read in the chapter.

And that brings us to this point in the book. There remains the Appendix, where you will find some useful sources of information:

- A variety of organizations and their websites, including government entities, teacher unions and professional organizations, as well as publishers who are currently producing books for TAs.
- A glossary of terms relating to education in general and the role of the TA in particular. Many of them occur somewhere in the body of the book, but a quick glance at the glossary will save you rummaging through the whole book to find them.

General principles for success

We have covered quite a range of topics in this book, but there are some general principles that run through many of the chapters, and that underpin your success as a TA:

- Communication. Open and honest communication is critical to your success. You need to communicate freely with the pupils you have been assigned, but you also need to communicate honestly with your supervising teacher and other adults you may work with. If you have concerns or are unclear about any of your supervisor's expectations, if you are uncomfortable about anything that you are asked to do, the only solution is to ask for clarification. But communication is also for the positive and enjoyable aspects of your work. Use it to let your supervisor know when he or she has been particularly helpful, or when you have gained useful insights from watching his or her interactions with pupils. You don't work in isolation, and good communication is one of the keys to effective collaboration.

■ Perspective. In all of your dealings with pupils and adults you need to stand back and view things in perspective. This includes being honest with yourself, and stopping frequently to make reality checks. There are certain undeniable facts about yourself and your work situation – you are young or old, experienced or inexperienced, well qualified or not – but taken in perspective these facts become more or less important. They can also be viewed as positive or negative depending on your perspective. Having few formal qualifications may seem like a disadvantage, but this is less important than being willing to learn. Having a great deal of experience is a great advantage, but perhaps more important is being prepared to keep an open mind and adapt to changing needs and preferences. So when you take a look at yourself and what is required of you as a TA, be honest about your capabilities, but also about what is required of you.

■ Personal responsibility. As an adult you are expected to take responsibility for yourself, and this is also something that we try to teach children from a young age. In your work as a TA you can also be proactive, and take responsibility for your own success and progress. You can ask for help rather than waiting for it to be offered; you can seek in-service training and formal qualifications; you can take up a personal programme of study if no other avenue for training is available; you can seek supervision and support from your supervising teacher even if he or she is not very proactive in this area. Essentially, the extent to which you are successful as a TA is largely up to you. Admittedly you may have an ineffective and unwilling supervisor, but fortunately those are in the minority. Most teachers are willing to provide whatever help you need to be effective in your work. There is a great deal you can do to enhance your capabilities as a TA. Do it. It is part of being a professional.

The diagram overleaf shows these three general principles as overlapping, rather than being independent of one another. As you take responsibility for your own learning and effectiveness, you will need to be open in your communications with your supervising teacher and others; you will also need to be honest and realistic about what it means to work alongside others and about what you can achieve together.

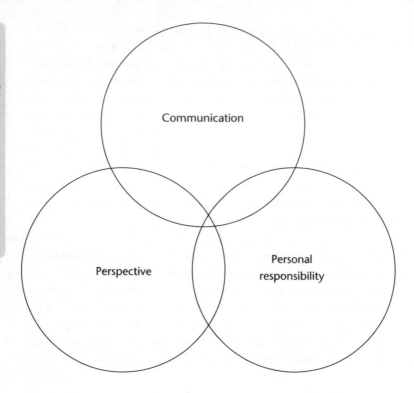

Figure 5.1: General principles governing your success as a TA

Where do you go from here?

Where you go from here is really up to you. Your continuing professional development can proceed at a pace that suits your temperament and the extent of your ambition. You may wish to let the information you have gained settle, and be put to good use for a while before considering where to go next. You may be so enthused by what you have learned that you can't wait to study some more and gain formal qualifications for your study. As you continue to study you may feel that you would like to qualify as a teacher, rather than continuing to work as a TA. Many TAs, particularly if they have embarked on a course of study that leads to formal qualifications, choose to go one step further and take the additional courses that give them Qualified Teacher Status. A qualification such as the Foundation Degree can usually be counted towards a teaching qualification.

Whichever option you choose, you will be taking steps towards increasing your effectiveness as a TA. This is a dynamic and ongoing process: as you encounter new situations, and work to support different pupils and teachers, you will increase your repertoire of teaching and behaviour management skills, and continue to gain valuable experience. These are critical skills for a TA. And underpinning this knowledge of methods and procedures, your success as a TA will also depend upon your having a clear understanding of your evolving roles and responsibilities as they change with each new school year, and your ongoing efforts to work effectively with your current supervising teacher.

Appendix

Useful sources of information and training

There are many sources of useful information relating to your work as a TA. These include:

- Your teacher and his or her resources/professional library. Most teachers have a shelf of books relating to teaching and classroom management strategies, as well as more specific topics such as dyslexia or developing children's thinking skills. Your supervising teacher may well be willing to let you dip into these resources.
- Your local college of higher education or university should offer courses in basic skills and ICT, as well as more specific training in education. Try a web search for course offerings or ask for course information at your local library.
- Other TAs. Take every opportunity which presents itself to network with other TAs and learn from them and their experience.
- Your local library will usually have a section on learning or child development. Many of the books are written for parents or carers, but they offer plenty of useful information for anyone who works with children or young people.

There are of course thousands of books on teaching and learning – textbooks and more user-friendly versions – but an increasing number of publishers are now producing books specifically for TAs. Easiest access to publishers' catalogues is through their websites. Here are some to start with:

- **David Fulton publishers**
  www.fultonpublishers.co.uk
  David Fulton is primarily a publisher of books relating to special needs. The books in the *Supporting Children* series were written for TAs working with pupils with special needs, and each one deals with a different aspect of disability (for example, autism or visual impairments). Fulton's *Helping Hands* series is written for TAs who support the development of literacy skills. If you search the website, using the term *teaching assistant*, you will find more than 30 books written specifically for TAs.

- **Sage Publications**
  www.sagepub.co.uk
  If you search the Sage website using the term *teaching assistant* you will find more than 20 books listed, among them *A Toolkit for the Effective Teaching Assistant* and *Supporting Children's Learning*. Although not all of them are written specifically for TAs, they make suitable reading for anyone supporting an inclusive learning environment.

- **Continuum**
  www.continuumbooks.com
  Continuum publishes books on a very wide range of topics, but if you click on 'View series titles' on the website home page you will find several series that relate to education: *Continuum One Hundreds*, *Special Educational Needs* and *Supporting Children* (this one specifically for TAs). In the general education catalogue you will also find *101 Essential Lists for Teaching Assistants*. Continuum is of course the publisher for this book, which is one of a new Teaching Assistant series. Books on a variety of topics relevant to TAs (literacy, how children learn, behaviour management, etc.) will be added to the series over the next few years, so keep an eye out for new titles, from Continuum as well as from other publishers.

Organizations and websites

This section is divided into three parts. The first two cover government organizations and professional organizations for teachers in the UK. These each present a different perspective on your role as a TA: the government websites present the official and legal view; the professional organizations often provide summaries of the legal documents, as well as a commentary on them. The third part of the section lists some organizations in the United States, where more than 1 million TAs are employed. Also listed are organizations in Australia and Canada.

Government organizations
Department for Education and Skills (DfES)
www.dfes.gov.uk
The DfES is the government department for education. Its website has links to a variety of documents and other useful information relating to TAs.

Teachernet
www.teachernet.gov.uk
As the name suggests, this is a website for teachers, but also for other school staff. If you go to the website and click on 'whole school issues', and then 'support staff' you will find links to government documents and guidance relating to TAs. Other interesting information on the site includes case studies, which give examples of good practice in using support staff in a variety of roles and in liaising with the community. There are also copies of training modules that schools in England can use to provide induction training to TAs, on topics such as behaviour management, child protection, ICT, Special Educational Needs and Inclusion. You will also find links to a *r* teacher associations and unions.

The Training and Development Agency for Schools
www.tda.gov.uk

The TDA was established to help schools 'develop the workforce', by providing training for teachers and other school staff. The responsibility for training TAs has been delegated to the School Workforce Development Board (SWDB). The Support Staff link on the TDA website takes you to the SWDB pages (www.tda.gov.uk/support/swdb.aspx) which describe the various qualifications that are now available to Teaching Assistants.

Local Government Employers (LGE)
www.lge.gov.uk

The LGE was set up in April 2006 to replace the Employers Organization (EO), and is considered the national centre of excellence for local authorities on pay, pensions and employment. The LGE website also has a considerable amount of information relating to TAs, which you can tap into by clicking on the link to *Education* once you get into the website. One of the recent additions to the website is the government document 'School Support Staff: The Way Forward' published in March 2006, which you can download (in PDF or Word) or read online.

The National Association of Professional Teaching Assistants (NAPTA)
www.napta.org.uk

NAPTA is a professional organization whose main focus is offering professional development resources to schools and LEAS. When an individual school pays the institutional membership fee, all support staff in the school receive individual membership and can then access resources through NAPTA's website. These include newsletters, summaries of government documents relating to TAs, and an 'Ask the Expert' service. NAPTA also offers a Workforce Development Programme. This is a package which helps schools evaluate their current use of support staff and then provides resources to meet their professional development needs.

Teacher unions and professional associations

There is a large number of organizations for teachers, many of which now offer membership to TAs and other support staff. The websites for these organizations all provide information about the current legislation relating to TAs, as well as updates on policies and government guidelines. As the documents are often summarized, this offers a more user-friendly and accessible way of gathering useful and interesting information. You can search these websites using keywords such as *teaching assistants*. Here's a selection of teacher associations and their websites:

Association of Teachers and Lecturers (ATL)
www.atl.org.uk

National Association of Schoolmasters Union of Women Teachers (NASUWT)
www.nasuwt.org.uk

National Association for Special Educational Needs (NASEN)
www.nasen.org.uk

National Union of Teachers (NUT)
www.teachers.org.uk

Professional Association of Teachers (PAT)
www.pat.org.uk

PAT includes PANN, the Professional Association of Nursery Nurses, and PAtT (Professionals Allied to Teaching i.e. support staff).

US organizations

The USA is the largest employer of Teaching Assistants, so you may be interested to find out more about what is happening for TAs on the other side of the Atlantic. Try this selection of websites for more information:

The National Resource Center for Paraprofessionals (NRCP)
www.nrcpara.org
The NRCP is the national organization representing TAs in America. Its website contains information on conferences, resources, projects relating to TAs in various States, and a chat room where TAs can exchange ideas and questions.

The National Education Association (NEA)
www.nea.org
The NEA is one of the two major teachers' unions in the United States and has information for TAs under the heading of Education Support Personnel (ESP).

The American Federation of Teachers (AFT)
www.aft.org
The AFT is the other major teachers' union in the United States and has pages relating to TAs under the heading of Paraprofessionals and School Related Personnel (PSRP).

The Council for Exceptional Children (CEC)
www.cec.sped.org
CEC is the largest organization in the United States representing children and youth with disabilities. As the majority of TAs in America are employed to support pupils with special needs, CEC has produced 'Performance Based Standards for Paraeducators' (TAs), and they can be found on the CEC website, as well as other information relating to TAs who work with children with special needs.

Australia and Canada
Australia
www.jobsearch.gov.au/joboutlook/
This site provides information on all occupations in Australia. Use the search term *teacher's aides* to find information on TAs.

Canada
www.jobfutures.ca
The search term *teacher assistant* will give you information about TAs working in schools, rather than *teaching assistant* which refers to those who work in higher education.

Glossary

This glossary provides definitions for a range of terms relating to your work as a Teaching Assistant.

Advanced Modern Apprenticeship (AMA)
The Advanced Modern Apprenticeship is a work-based qualification, intended for TAs who work under the direction of a teacher, but who contribute to planning, implementing and evaluating learning activities – in other words, those who have greater responsibilities and are able to work more independently. The basic components are the same as for the Foundation Modern Apprenticeship (FMA – see below), but qualifications must be at a higher level (e.g. Level 3 NVQ rather than Level 2 for the FMA).

Aide
Term used formerly in the USA to denote TAs or other support staff. This term became less popular with the increase in AIDS, and has been replaced with a variety of more descriptive titles for TAs, such as paraeducator, instructional assistant or education technician.

Education Act
The Education Act came into law in England and Wales in July 2002, and its aims are to implement the government's commitments to education as set out in the White Paper 'Schools – Achieving Success'. According to the Department for Education and Skills, the Act will 'raise standards,

promote innovation in schools and reform education law'. You can find more detail on the DfES website (www.dfes.gov.uk/educationact2002).

Foundation Degree for Teaching Assistants

Foundation Degrees are available in a variety of fields. The essential and common factor is that the student must be employed in the appropriate field while studying for the degree, as the Foundation Degree is based on the concept of work-based learning. Foundation Degree courses are offered on a part-time basis to allow for the student's work schedule, and for course assignments to be completed in relation to the TA's current work placement. More information about Foundation Degrees in England and Wales can be found on the website www.fdf.ac.uk.

Foundation Modern Apprenticeship (FMA)

The FMA is a vocational qualification available for a variety of occupations, including Teaching Assistant. It consists of several components: basic skills (literacy and numeracy), NVQs, and a technical qualification such as a BTEC in an appropriate subject. Unlike previous apprenticeship schemes which had an upper age limit, Modern Apprenticeships are open to all age groups. Foundation MAs are intended for TAs who have limited responsibilities, and who work under the close supervision of a teacher who plans the lessons and provides daily direction. See also Advanced Modern Apprenticeship.

Higher Level Teaching Assistant (HLTA)

The most advanced level of TA designated by the government. In order to attain HLTA status, a TA must demonstrate competence in various areas relating to teaching and classroom management. This is done through a portfolio of written assignments which describe teaching experiences and how they demonstrate understanding of each of the competences. There is also an interview to assess the TAs knowledge and understanding.

Individual Education Plan (IEP)
A document drawn up for each child with a disability in UK schools, consisting of a description of the child's abilities and challenges, goals and objectives for improvement, the specific support that will be provided to enable the child to access the curriculum, and where appropriate, an individualized behavioural plan. The IEP is a legal contract between the LA and the child/parents, and can be challenged if it is felt to be inappropriate, or inadequately adhered to. The IEP was formerly known as a Statement (of educational needs). In the USA, the IEP is known as an Individualized Education Program.

Learning Support Assistant (LSA)
A term previously used by the UK government for support staff, but since replaced with Teaching Assistant.

National Vocational Qualifications (NVQs)
NVQs are work-related qualifications, based on the National Occupational Standards for a particular occupation, such as Teaching Assistant. The standards consist of statements describing the skills and knowledge that show a person is competent for their work.

Qualifications and Curriculum Authority (QCA)
This is a DfES-sponsored organization, responsible for developing the national curriculum, SATs and other exams, and monitoring qualifications at higher education level and in the workplace. National Vocational Qualfications (NVQs) come under the remit of the QCA. For more information see www.qca.org.uk

No Child Left Behind
Although this phrase is sometimes used by politicians in the

UK to mark their commitment to education, it originates in the United States. It is the popular title for the 2001 re-authorization of the Elementary and Secondary Education Act in the USA. No Child Left Behind has had a considerable effect on TAs in America, as it requires them to have qualifications equivalent to two years of full-time college, or pass a rigourous test showing that they have the skills and knowledge to teach reading, writing and mathematics. Although these requirements are officially only for TAs supporting literacy and numeracy programmes for disadvantaged children (known as Title I programmes), the effect is much more widespread because all TAs working in a school that receives funding for Title I programmes must have the higher qualifications.

Paraprofessional
Another term for Teaching Assistants, used in some places in the UK, and the official term used in government legislation in the US.

School Workforce Development Board (SWDB)
The SWDB is the sector-wide body (for education) concerned with training and development for support staff. It consists of representatives from national bodies such as the DfES, Ofsted and the QCA. In early 2006 it published a three-year plan for training and developing school support staff.

SENDA
This is the Special Educational Needs and Disability Act which came into law in 2002 and is designed to protect the legal rights of pupils from pre-school right through to post-16 education. The most basic right of pupils with special needs is not to be discriminated against in education and training (or related services such as exams, libraries and learning resources). More information can be found on the Skill website (www.skill.org.uk). Skill is the National Bureau for Students with Disabilities.